D1585686

LAW
BASICS
Student Study Guides

UNJUSTIFIED ENRICHMENT

THIRD EDITION

LAW
BASICS
Student Study Guides

UNJUSTIFIED ENRICHMENT

THIRD EDITION

By

Hector MacQueen

Scottish Law Commissioner
and Professor of Private Law, University of Edinburgh

W. GREEN   THOMSON REUTERS

First Edition published 2004
Second Edition published 2009
Reprinted 2010

Published in 2013 by W. Green, 21 Alva Street, Edinburgh EH2 4PS
part of Thomson Reuters (Professional) UK Limited
(Registered in England & Wales, Company No 1679046.
Registered Office and address for service:
2nd Floor, 1 Mark Square, Leonard Street, London EC2A 4EG)

Typeset by W. Green, Edinburgh
Printed and bound in Great Britain by
CPI Group (UK) Ltd, Croydon, CR0 4YY

No natural forests were destroyed to make this product:
only farmed timber was used and re-planted.

A CIP catalogue record for this book is available from the British
Library.

ISBN 978-0-414-01909-6

PREFACE TO THE THIRD EDITION

The fourth incarnation of this text (which began life as a chapter in a textbook on general Scots law ten years ago) has required less revision than its two immediate predecessors. There has not been so much significant new case law, and the general principles and approach which were to at least some extent speculative back in 2003 now seem to have gained a degree of acceptance. The main issue in the Scottish courts now is not so much the idea that enrichments are unjustified and must be reversed when supported by no legal ground, more getting the judges (and the lawyers arguing before them) to take on board that the inquiry into "justification" and "legal grounds" must also go into the question of whether cases fall into one or other of the categories labelled in this book as enrichment by transfer, enrichment by imposition and enrichment by taking. If we look only at the general principle, possibly informed by notions that enrichment is an "equitable" area of law, we face the danger, identified by the great American comparatist John P. Dawson in his famous book *Unjust Enrichment* (1952), that judges will either "jump off the dock" (p.8) or "rocket up into the stratosphere" (even if in the latter scenario they first "fasten their seat belts") (p.12). This may have disastrous results for the predictability and certainty of the law, with recovery denied in cases where it should have been allowed, or allowed where it should have been denied. Perhaps legal analysis will be improved once Robin Evans-Jones' *magnum opus* is completed by the publication of its second volume later this year, with reinforcement in prospect when Niall Whitty completes his eagerly anticipated chapter on unjustified enrichment for the *Stair Memorial Encyclopaedia*. In the meantime, this little book may help point the legal practitioners of the future away from the dock and the stratosphere into which their seniors may currently be tempted to jump or soar, as the case may be.

I am once again deeply indebted to friends who have shared with me their insights on enrichment law: Niall Whitty, Martin Hogg, Jacques du Plessis and Dot Reid have all generously transferred their latest thinking, only rarely sought to impose, and have posed no obstacles to my takings from the body of their thought.

I dedicate the book again to Patrick, now enriching himself on a legal basis in the southern hemisphere and possibly managing to benefit his hosts at least a little as well.

Hector MacQueen
April 2013
Causewayside, Edinburgh

PREFACE TO THE SECOND EDITION

In this second edition I have set out to update the text published in 2004, while also taking the opportunity to restructure some of the material to clarify and develop the treatment of certain topics, notably the *condictio sine causa*, enrichment by taking, subsidiarity and remedies. I have gained much from further research on other mixed legal systems, notably South Africa and Louisiana, and have benefited also from engagement with Book VII (Unjustified Enrichment) of the Draft Common Frame of Reference published first in 2008 and then again, in a revised edition, in 2009.

I remain deeply indebted to the many colleagues and friends with whom I have continued to discuss unjustified enrichment; in particular again Niall Whitty and Martin Hogg. I have learned much from supervising the doctoral work of Saul Miller and Dot Reid. I also thank Jill Urquhart for her much appreciated toil in ordering the heap of materials on enrichment law accumulated in my Old College office over many years. This was of great help in preparing this second edition.

The book continues to be dedicated to Patrick, now enriching the world of human resources management.

Hector MacQueen
March 2009
Old College
University of Edinburgh

PREFACE TO THE FIRST EDITION

This short book reproduces a slightly updated version of what began life as Chapter 8 of *Fundamentals of Scots Law*, first published in 2003. It now has the advantage of being set against the background of the much more detailed treatment in Robin Evans-Jones *Unjustified Enrichment: Volume 1: Enrichment by Deliberate Conferral: Condictio*, published in the Scottish Universities Law Institute series later in 2003, and also takes account of some recent sheriff court and Outer House decisions.

I remain grateful to the many colleagues and friends with whom I have discussed unjustified enrichment over the years; in particular in connection with this book, Niall Whitty (whose own treatment of the topic is eagerly anticipated), David Sellar and Martin Hogg. It is 20 years since Peter Birks first made me realise that the Scots law of enrichment would repay comparative study, and I would like to take this opportunity to acknowledge, with gratitude, his unfailing example of inquiry and intellectual rigour in the study of law.

The book is dedicated to Patrick, in the hope that all his enrichments will be justified ones.

June 2004

CONTENTS

TABLE OF CASES

TABLE OF STATUTES

TABLE OF STATUTORY INSTRUMENTS

1. INTRODUCTION

WHAT IS MEANT BY UNJUSTIFIED ENRICHMENT?

The basic idea of the law of unjustified enrichment, which first began to emerge long ago in Roman law,[1] is that a person who has been unjustifiedly enriched at another's expense must restore the enrichment to that other.[2] At first sight, this seems odd: one of the fundamental tenets of Western society is the lawfulness of making yourself richer—even if that involves loss to another—as, for example, when I compete successfully with you in business, so that I make profits and you lose customers you used to have. More violent, dishonest or other similar methods of enriching yourself at another's expense, such as robbery, theft and fraud, are of course prohibited by the criminal law. But Scots civil (or private) law (like most modern legal systems) recognises that some enrichments, arising in contexts going beyond the criminal ones just mentioned, are also unjustified, so that the enriched person has to give it back to the person at whose expense it was obtained, or, if restoration is not possible, pay for the enrichment.

Three key concepts triggering the obligation to give enrichment back are, therefore:

- enrichment of one party (the defender); see further below, Chap.2;
- at the expense of another party (the pursuer); see further below, Chap.3; and
- unjustified for the first party to retain the enrichment; see further below, Chap.4.

It is the job of the law to define each of these concepts, so that parties, lawyers and courts can have a reasonably clear idea when the obligation arises and, equally or even more important, when it does not. Essentially, this comes down to working out what justice requires, but it is important to realise that this working out has been done, and continues to have to be done, in accordance with principles and rules contained in the definitions of the law's fundamental concepts—and not just as an instinctive or intuitive response to the various enrichment situations which life throws up from time to time.

For this reason, the better name of our subject is unjustified, rather than unjust, enrichment (a usage which is nonetheless found in both texts and cases).[3] As the point has been well expressed by one writer:

---

[1] See *Digest* 12.6.14; 50.17.206 (for this by nature is equitable, that no-one be enriched at the expense of another).

[2] This is recognised as the "basic rule" of unjustified enrichment in DCFR VII.-1:101 (DCFR references follow "Book, Chapter, Article" throughout, therefore the above reference points to Book 7, Chap.1, art.101).

[3] The name "quasi-contract" will often be found in older materials, but has been abandoned in the modern law as misleading about the nature of the subject.

"'Unjustified' is more accurate, though less specific. 'Unjust' normally refers to a moral criterion. So if it is used in the present context a lot of effort has to go into explaining that it does not mean unjust in the normal sense but has a very special and unusual meaning."[1]

THE DEVELOPMENT OF SCOTS LAW

Until the 1990s, the approach of Scots law was to start analysis of this subject under three headings, as follows:

- **repetition**—claims for the return of money;
- **restitution**—claims for the return of other forms of property; and
- **recompense**—claims for other benefits resulting from the expenditure or actings of the pursuer.

Under each of these headings were defined the categories of enrichments which the law recognised as unjustified. In the actions of repetition and restitution in particular, Scots law used Roman law to help it make these definitions. Roman law too divided enrichment law up into a series of actions, the most important of which were known as the *conditiones*.[2] For our purposes the most significant of these are:

- *condictio indebiti* (action for return of an undue payment);
- *condictio causa data causa non secuta* (action for return of a payment rendered for a purpose which failed to materialise);
- *condictio ob injustam vel turpem causam* (action for return of payment rendered for an illegal or immoral purpose);
- *condictio sine causa* (action for return of a payment which the defender has no legal basis for retaining against the pursuer); and
- *condictio ob causam finitam* (a form of the *condictio sine causa*; action for return of payment which had a legal basis when made but that has now ceased to exist).

These Latin phrases were employed in the Scottish cases of repetition and restitution to explain which enrichments should, or should not, be reversed. In cases of recompense, however, there was no reference to the *conditiones*.[3] Instead recompense appeared to cover cases of enrichment not falling within the categories of repetition and restitution, but where nonetheless it was held that there should be recovery. Examples included the provision of services, such as improvements to another's property, or other cases where exact return of the enrichment transferred was not possible, but a benefit, which ought to be paid for, had clearly occurred.

---

[1]   E.M. Clive, *Draft Rules on Unjustified Enrichment and Commentary*, Appendix to Scottish Law Commission Discussion Paper No.99 (1996), pp.19–20.

[2]   See *Digest* 12.4 (*causa data causa non secuta*); 12.5 (*ob turpem vel injustam causam*); 12.6 (*indebiti*); 12.7 (*sine causa*); 12.7.2 (*ob causam finitam*).

[3]   The *actio de in rem verso* (*Code* 4, 26, 7, 3), also received in Scots law, may have played its part in the development of recompense.

A NEW APPROACH

The approach outlined above was much criticised by academic writers and others from the 1980s on.[1] Was there any reason for distinguishing between repetition and restitution? What, if any, were the limits of recompense and how did it relate to the other actions? Was it a subsidiary general action picking up those cases of enrichment which the other actions did not reach? Would it not be better, and more in accordance with the principled nature of Scots law, to start by defining the subject from the events which triggered liability—unjustified enrichments—rather than with the available remedial responses? The Scottish Law Commission brought enrichment law under detailed consideration in the 1990s. After this began, however, the courts started to move away from the traditional approach outlined above, and to adopt a more general yet systematic way of looking at the subject, based on the idea of an obligation to restore or pay for unjustified enrichment at another's expense. The key cases are *Morgan Guaranty Trust Co of New York v Lothian Regional Council*[2] and, in particular, *Shilliday v Smith*.[3] The facts and decisions of these cases will be discussed later in the book, but here we focus on the general approach to enrichment established by the judgments in them. In *Morgan Guaranty* Lord President Hope emphasised the need for a unified approach to the subject in a decision abolishing the exclusion of error in law as a ground for the recovery of a payment to another (see further below, pp.26–31).

> "The important point is that these actions [of repetition, restitution and recompense] are all means to the same end, which is to redress an unjustified enrichment upon the broad equitable principle *nemo debet locupletari aliena jactura*. Thus the action of repetition, to take this as an example, may be based upon the *condictio causa data causa non secuta*, the *condictio sine causa* or the *condictio indebiti* depending upon which of these grounds of action fits the circumstances which give rise to the claim. The nature of the benefit received by the defender and the circumstances on which the pursuer relies for his claim ought, in a properly organised structure for this branch of the law, to provide all that is needed for the selection of the appropriate remedy. The selection is distorted if there is introduced into the structure a rule [the error of law rule] which is essentially one of expediency rather than of equity between the parties … It becomes wholly disorganised if that rule is applied to one of the remedies within the system and not to others, with the result that a pursuer is driven to seeking another less appropriate remedy to escape from it."

Per Lord President Hope at 155.

---

[1] See H.L. MacQueen, "Peter Birks and Scots enrichment law", in *Mapping the Law: Essays in Memory of Peter Birks*, A. Burrows and Lord Rodger of Earlsferry (eds) (2006).
[2] *Morgan Guaranty Trust Co of New York v Lothian Regional Council*, 1995 S.C. 151.
[3] *Shilliday v Smith*, 1998 S.C. 725.

Shilliday is most important for the general approach to the whole subject outlined by the Lord President, Lord Rodger of Earlsferry.

> "A person may be said to be unjustly enriched at another's expense when he has obtained a benefit from the other's actings or expenditure, without there being a legal ground which would justify him in retaining that benefit. The significance of one person being unjustly enriched at the expense of another is that in general terms it constitutes an event which triggers a right in that other person to have the enrichment reversed.
>
> As the law has developed, it has identified various situations where persons are to be regarded as having been unjustly enriched at another's expense and where the person may accordingly seek to have the enrichment reversed. The authorities show that some of these situations fall into recognisable groups or categories. Since these situations correspond, if only somewhat loosely, to situations where remedies were granted in Roman law, in referring to the relevant categories our law tends to use the terminology which is found in the Digest and Code. The terms include *condictio indebiti, condictio causa data causa non secuta*, and, to a lesser extent, *condictio sine causa*.
>
> Once he has satisfied himself that he has a relevant case, anyone contemplating bringing an action must then determine how the court is to reverse the defender's enrichment if it decides in the pursuer's favour. This will depend on the particular circumstances. The person framing the pleadings must consider how the defender's enrichment has come about and then search among the usual range of remedies to find a remedy or combination of remedies which will achieve his purpose of having that enrichment reversed.
>
> Elementary examples make this clear. For instance, if A has been unjustly enriched because he has received a sum of money from B, the enrichment can be reversed by ordering A to repay the money to B. B's remedy will be repetition of the sum of money from A. On the other hand, if the unjust enrichment arises out of the transfer of moveable property, the enrichment can be reversed by ordering A to transfer the property back to B. An action of restitution of the property will be appropriate ... If A is unjustly enriched by having had the benefit of B's services, the enrichment can be reversed by ordering A to pay B a sum representing the value of the benefit which A has enjoyed. An action of recompense will be appropriate. So repetition, restitution ... and recompense are simply examples of remedies which the courts grant to reverse an unjust enrichment, depending on the way in which the particular enrichment has arisen."

Per Lord President Rodger at 727, 728.

This was also approved by Lord Hope of Craighead in the subsequent House of Lords case, *Dollar Land (Cumbernauld) Ltd v CIN Properties Ltd.*[1]

"These actions [of repetition, restitution and recompense] were all means to the same end, which is to address an unjustified enrichment … For my part I see no harm in the continued use of these expressions to describe the various remedies, so long as it is understood that they are being used merely to describe the nature of the remedy which the court is being asked to provide in order to redress the enrichment. The event which gives rise to the granting of the remedy is the enrichment. In general terms it may be said that the remedy is available where the enrichment lacks a legal ground to justify the retention of the benefit. In such circumstances it is held to be unjust."

Per Lord Hope at 98.

As a result of these cases, Scots law has now reached a position where, in principle, an enrichment is said to be unjustified and therefore should be reversed if its retention is supported by no legal ground.[2] Examples of "legal grounds", or justifications, for enrichments include receipt under a gift or in performance of a valid contract, as well as gain through lawful competition in the market place, already mentioned above. On the other side of the coin, the *condictiones* should be seen as descriptions of situations in which an enrichment of any kind would be seen as unjustified, while repetition (repayment of money), restitution (restoration of property), and recompense (payment for the service or other enrichment rendered) are remedies which the court can grant once it has decided that an enrichment is unjustified. But neither the *condictiones*, nor the ground covered in the past by the traditional remedies, exhaust the ways in which the courts may find or reverse unjustified enrichment: this is the significance of accepting the general principle requiring the reversal of unjustified enrichment.[3]

Scots law on this subject is, therefore, still in a state of development and consequently some uncertainty, although the Scottish Law Commission has decided that in the light of the 1990s cases reforming legislation is no longer necessary, and that the law can be left for development by the courts and textbook writers. Professor Robin Evans-Jones of Aberdeen produced in 2003 the first part of what is planned to be

---

[1] *Dollar Land (Cumbernauld) Ltd v CIN Properties Ltd*, 1998 S.C. (H.L.) 90 at 98.

[2] In reaching this position Scots law seems to be moving in the same general direction as that advocated for English law in P. Birks, *Unjust Enrichment*, 2nd edn (see further below, pp.40–41) as well as that pursued by the Supreme Court of Canada under the banner "absence of juristic reason" (*Garland v Consumers Gas Co* (2004) 1 S.C.R. 629). The DCFR VII.-2:101(1) states that an enrichment is unjustified unless the enriched person is entitled to it by virtue of a contract or other juridical act, court order or rule of law.

[3] See, e.g. *Macadam v Grandison* [2008] CSOH 53, per Lord Hodge, para.35; *Mactaggart & Mickel Homes Ltd v Hunter* [2010] CSOH 130, per Lord Hodge, paras 98–100.

a two-volume work on the subject of unjustified enrichment. This volume deals in detail with the application of the *condictiones*; the second will consider other elements of enrichment law.[1] A broad framework for approaching enrichment has thus emerged—but the full implications of this reorientation for the existing case law and the shaping of future decisions are, at this stage, still a matter on which textbook writers must speculate to some degree.

There has, however, been a growing consensus amongst legal writers as to the underlying principles of the law and the approach that needs to be taken, and this book seeks to reflect something of that consensus.[2] It is structured around the three basic concepts of the defender's enrichment, at the expense of the pursuer, and the factors making this situation unjustified and in need of remedy. The book then briefly considers the defences available to the enriched person, and the remedies that can be granted by the court. However, the reader should be aware that there are still gaps in the law, perhaps inevitably in an uncodified system, and that the introductory account given here will be subject to elaboration and correction in the light of further decisions and analysis.

Much is already to be learned, however, and gaps may be filled, by considering the experience of other European legal systems, and also that of South Africa, like Scotland a mixed jurisdiction. Developments in the rather different law of England may give some insights as to problems likely to arise also in Scotland. The unjustified enrichment book of the Draft Common Frame of Reference ("DCFR"), published in 2009, provides a further well-articulated model for Scots lawyers to consider and use in the development of their own law as well as an indicator of the shape of a future European enrichment law.

FURTHER READING

On the history of enrichment law in Scotland, see H.L. MacQueen and W.D.H. Sellar, "Unjust enrichment in Scots law" in *Unjust Enrichment: The Comparative Legal History of the Law of Restitution*, edited by E.J.H. Schrage (1995); R. Evans-Jones, "Unjustified enrichment" in *History of Private Law in Scotland*, edited by K.G.C. Reid and R. Zimmermann (2000), Vol.2; H.L. MacQueen, "Peter Birks and Scots enrichment law", in *Mapping the Law: Essays in Memory of Peter Birks*, edited by A. Burrows and Lord Rodger of Earlsferry (2006); and D. Reid, "Thomas Aquinas and Viscount Stair: the influence of scholastic moral theology on Stair's account of restitution and recompense" (2008) 29 *Journal of Legal History* 189. This should be seen against the general

---

[1] R. Evans-Jones, *Unjustified Enrichment: Enrichment by Deliberate Conferral: Condictio* (2003). Publication of the second volume is anticipated in 2014.

[2] See e.g. R. Zimmermann, D. Visser and K. Reid (eds) *Mixed Legal Systems in Comparative Perspective: Property and Obligations in Scotland and South Africa* (2005), Chs 14–16; M.A. Hogg, *Obligations* 2nd edn (2006), pp.195–241; Gloag & Henderson *The Law of Scotland* 13th edn (2012), Ch.24.

Roman law and European background, for which see R. Zimmermann, *The Law of Obligations: Roman Foundations of the Civil Law Tradition* (1990), Ch.26.

The discussion of law reform by the Scottish Law Commission, in its Discussion Papers Nos 95 (1993), 99 and 100 (1996) and the resulting *Report on Unjustified Enrichment: Error of Law and Public Authority Receipts and Disbursements* (Scot. Law Com. No.169, February 1999), contained much influential analysis of the pre-*Shilliday* authorities. For assessment of the impact of *Shilliday* (along with *Morgan Guaranty* and *Dollar Land*) see, e.g. P. Hellwege, "Rationalising the Scottish law of unjustified enrichment" (2000) 11 *Stellenbosch L.R.* 50; two articles by M.A. Hogg: "Lowlands to Low Countries: perspectives on the Scottish and Dutch law of unjustified enrichment", *Ius Commune Lectures in European Private Law, No.3* (2001), and "Unjustified enrichment in Scots law twenty years on: where now?" [2006] R.L.R. 1; W.D.H. Sellar, "*Shilliday v Smith*: unjustified enrichment through the looking glass" (2001) 5 *Edinburgh L.R.* 80, and two articles by N.R. Whitty: "The Scottish enrichment revolution" (2001) 6 *Scottish Law & Practice Quarterly* 167, and "Rationality, nationality, and the taxonomy of unjustified enrichment", in *Unjustified Enrichment: Key Issues in Comparative Perspective*, edited by D. Johnston and R. Zimmermann (2002), Ch.23.

For *comparative perspectives on enrichment law*, see P. Schlechtriem, C. Coen and R. Hornung, "Restitution and unjust enrichment in Europe" (2001) 9 *European Review of Private Law* 377 and J. du Plessis, "Comparison and evaluation: lessons from enrichment law" (2012) 76 *Rabels Zeitschrift* 947. For South African law, see D.P. Visser, *Unjustified Enrichment* (2008) and J. du Plessis, *The South African Law of Unjustified Enrichment* (2012). Scots and South African law are compared as mixed systems in *Mixed Legal Systems in Comparative Perspective: Property and Obligations in Scotland and South Africa*, R. Zimmermann, D. Visser and K. Reid (eds), and in J. du Plessis, "Towards a rational structure of liability for unjustified enrichment: thoughts from two mixed jurisdictions", (2004) 121 *South African Law Journal* 142 (also published in *Grundstrukturen eines Europäischen Bereicherungsrechts* R. Zimmermann (ed) (2005), while a comparison between Scots and Louisiana law is made in H.L. MacQueen, "Unjustified enrichment, subsidiarity and contract", in *Mixed Jurisdictions Compared: Private Law in Louisiana and Scotland*, V.V. Palmer and E. Reid (eds) (2009). A more general comparison may be found in H.L. MacQueen, "Unjustified enrichment in mixed legal systems" (2005) 13 R.L.R. 21. The most accessible detailed account of English law is A. Burrows, *The Law of Restitution*, 3rd edn (2011). Burrows has also produced *A Restatement of the English Law of Restitution* (2012). Contrast, however, the very different perspectives in P. Birks, *Unjust Enrichment*, 2nd edn (2005) and S. Hedley, *A Critical Introduction to Restitution* (2001). Hedley also runs an invaluable restitution website including Scots law and other comparative materials: *http://www.ucc.ie/law/restitution/* [accessed January 29, 2013].

An English journal offering a wide comparative perspective, and again including Scots law, is the *Restitution Law Review (R.L.R.)*. A comparative casebook is E. Schrage and J. Beatson (eds), ***Cases, Materials and Texts on Unjustified Enrichment*** (2003) (Scottish contribution by W.D.H. Sellar and M.A. Hogg). For the Draft Common Frame of Reference see C. von Bar, E.M. Clive and H. Schulte-Nölke (eds), ***Principles, Definitions and Model Rules of European Private Law Outline Edition*** (2009).

---

2. ENRICHMENT

WHAT CONSTITUTES ENRICHMENT?

Enrichment is the receipt or acquisition of a benefit of economic worth, leading either to an increase in the person's wealth or to the avoidance of loss of wealth. The DCFR provides a neat summary perfectly applicable to Scots law:

> "A person is enriched by:
> • an increase in assets or a decrease in liabilities;
> • receiving a service or having work done;
> • use of another's assets."[1]

Receipt or acquisition of money
The classic case of such a benefit is the *receipt or acquisition of money*, and most of the cases in enrichment law are about that subject. See, for example:

Royal Bank of Scotland v Watt
1991 S.C. 48

W was a window-cleaner who had a bank account with RBS. W met T in a pub. T possessed a cheque drawn on the account of a well-known firm of solicitors, apparently for the amount of £18,631. T wanted to cash the cheque, but told W he lacked a bank account with which to do this. W offered to help T. The cheque was paid into W's account at the RBS, and he then withdrew the cash equivalent from the bank and gave it to T. W never saw T again, and it turned out that the cheque, originally for only £631, had been fraudulently altered. W had thus received cash from RBS, i.e. he was enriched at the bank's expense (since it could not enforce the cheque against the solicitors). W was found liable to repay the full amount.

---

[1]   DCFR VII.-3:101.

Morgan Guaranty Trust Co of New York
v Lothian Regional Council
1995 S.C. 151

LRC was a local authority and MG a merchant bank. The parties had entered into a contract under which MG made payments to LRC, which would be repaid in certain market conditions. It turned out that the contract was void. LRC had money from MG without any legal basis for its retention, i.e. the authority was enriched at the bank's expense, and it was found liable to repay the bank.

Receipt or acquisition of other property
The benefit may also be other forms of property, such as *goods or corporeal moveables* (the most common case after money), land, or some incorporeal property right. See, for example:

Findlay v Monro
(1698) Mor. 1767

F sent an ox to Macfarlane, but by mistake it was delivered to M. M thought that the ox was a gift from a friend, killed the beast and salted the carcase for consumption. It was held that M was enriched by receipt of the animal and was liable for that. (See further below, p.56, on the remedy.)

Receipt or acquisition of intangible benefits
Enrichment can also arise through the *receipt or acquisition of intangible benefits*, like the provision of a service which leaves no end product, as such, with the recipient (for example, the oral provision of advice, cleaning windows or polishing shoes).

ELCAP v Milne's Executor
1999 S.L.T. 58

M was an NHS patient receiving free care in a hospital when it was taken over by a charitable company ("E") and became a nursing home. In-patients not requiring continuing medical care were supposed, thereafter, to pay a charge to E. M was discharged as not requiring continuing medical care but continued to be cared for by E until his death three years later, although his *curator bonis* refused to pay the charges claimed by E. E's claim for recompense from M's estate for services rendered was held to be relevant (a case on implied contract was rejected, however).

Improvement of property
Sometimes enrichment arises because the recipient's *property is improved* in some way by another—for example, a building is repaired or renovated,

either increasing the property's market value, or saving the owner having to spend money on doing the work if the repairs were necessary ones. But the improvement may go beyond repair and maintenance, and extend to enhancement (sometimes termed "meliorations" in the cases), as for example erecting completely new buildings, or draining and cultivating land. However, improvements which are merely the provision of luxuries—for example, putting statues up in somebody else's garden—are not treated as enrichments.[1] Although land is the usual kind of property involved in the reported improvement cases, there is no reason why the subject-matter may not be corporeal moveables or, indeed, incorporeals.

See, for example:

Newton v Newton
1925 S.C. 715

H bought a house in the name of his prospective wife ("W"), in which the parties lived after their marriage. H, who honestly believed that he was the owner of the house, spent £400 on improving and repairing it. After the marriage broke down and it had been found that W, as owner, was entitled to continue to live in the house and exclude H from it, W was found to be enriched by having the benefit of H's improvements.

Shilliday v Smith
1998 S.C. 725

M and W began to live together in M's cottage in 1988, and became engaged in August 1990. They never married. In 1988, M had bought a house in a state of disrepair, and from about 1990 M and W began to improve this property, into which they moved together in 1991. The works were completed by Christmas 1992, when M ejected W from the house. W had spent about £9,600 on the works: approximately £7,000 direct to tradesmen whom she had instructed; £1,880 to M to pay for materials and work on the house, and £756 on items for the garden, left behind after her ejection. M was found to be enriched by W's payments to him and the workmen, which had led to the renovation of his property, and by the items she had left in the garden.

York Buildings Company v Mackenzie
(1795) 3 Pat. 378; (1797) 3 Pat. 579

YBC's estates were sold under court authority to M, who erected a mansionhouse, sank coal-mines and laid out plantations and policies on the ground. Eleven years later, YBC successfully reduced the sale. *Held*: that YBC was enriched by M's operations.

---

[1] See Bankton, *Institute of the Laws of Scotland*, 1.9.42.

Edinburgh Life Assurance Co v Balderston
(1909) 2 S.L.T. 323

A life assurance policy was kept in force by payment of premiums by assignees under an invalid assignation from the assured. *Held*: that the assignees had maintained another's property in good faith, thereby creating a benefit for that other.

Nortje en 'n Ander v Pool
1966 (3) S.A. 96 (A.)

In this South African case, a landowner ("E") and a prospector ("I") entered into a written agreement to the effect that I would be allowed to prospect for, and mine if found, kaolin on E's land. As a result of I's prospecting activities, which cost him R800, considerable quantities of kaolin were found on the land; but before mining could begin, the written agreement was found to be void, and E turned I off the ground. The land was now worth R15,000 more than it was before the discovery of the kaolin. Was E enriched? The South African court held not, but the general principle against unjustified enrichment in Scots law might suggest that the prospector I should have a claim. The case might be stronger if: (i) immediately after the discovery of the kaolin but before finding that the agreement with I was void, E sold the land to T, realising the enhancement of its value; or if (ii) E commenced mining operations and began to make large profits from the sale of kaolin; or if (iii) E, having commenced profitable mining operations, then sold the land and the mining business, realising large profits.

Unauthorised use of another's property

Again, there can be enrichment arising from the *unauthorised use of someone else's property*. Here again the enrichment is by way of a saving, in not having had to pay for that use hitherto. Thus, in the leading case of *Earl of Fife v Wilson*[1] W had possession of land under a lease which was found to be invalid against F, the heir of entail in the land; W was held to be enriched by his possession. In more recent cases, tenants who stayed on after the lease had been lawfully terminated before its full term had expired, were similarly found liable to the landlord for their unauthorised use.[2]

GTW Holdings Ltd v Toet
1994 S.L.T. (Sh.Ct) 16

T occupied land owned by GTW for five years, without any title to do so and without the owners knowing of the occupation. T was held to be

---

[1] *Earl of Fife v Wilson* (1867) 3 M. 323.
[2] *Glasgow District Council v Morrison McChlery & Co*, 1985 S.C. 52 (compulsory purchase of leased property); *HMV Fields Properties Ltd v Skirt' n' Slack Centre of London Ltd*, 1987 S.L.T. 2 (lease irritated).

enriched to the extent of the annual worth of the land over the period.

There may also be enrichment in cases where the owner allows another to occupy land, but the circumstances show that the occupation was not intended to be gratuitous.

Glen v Roy
(1882) 10 R. 239

A father consented to his son's possession of a house without putting a formal lease in place, but the son was found liable to pay for the enrichment arising from his occupation, having failed to show any intention of the father to make a gift to him, and it being presumed that a person who occupies another's land does so as tenant.

Shetland Islands Council v BP Petroleum Development Ltd
1990 S.L.T. 82

S Council allowed BP to occupy land which it owned, in order to construct an oil terminal (Sullum Voe). For several years the parties negotiated a lease of the land, while BP conducted operations from the site, but the negotiations were unsuccessful. *Held*: that BP could, in these circumstances, be made liable to the extent of the annual worth of the land.

Rochester Poster Services Ltd v AG Barr Plc
1994 S.L.T. (Sh.Ct) 2

AGB leased an advertising board site in Glasgow from RPS. The lease expired at the end of 1992 and negotiations for its renewal were unsuccessful; but AGB continued to advertise at the site for 17 months after the expiry of the lease. AGB was held to be enriched to the extent of the annual worth of the site over the 17-month period.

This enrichment by use of another's property can extend beyond land to *moveables*.[1] With moveables, the types of enriching use can be quite varied. Thus, for example, the possessor may make a profit by reselling the moveable to a third party.[2] Or, the possessor may consume or otherwise destroy the moveable,[3] or through action with it, involving the property doctrines of accession, commixtion, confusion or specification,[4] either gain ownership himself or confer it on a third party.[5] The following cases illustrate the types of situation that can arise (although note that what is recoverable by the pursuer varies according to the different fact situations, as discussed later in this book (see below, pp.56–58)).

---

[1] See, e.g. *Chisholm v Alexander* (1882) 19 S.L.R. 835.
[2] *Scot v Low* (1704) Mor. 9123; *Jarvis v Manson*, 1954 S.L.T. (Sh. Ct) 93.
[3] *Findlay v Monro* (1698) Mor. 1767; *Walker v Spence and Carfrae* (1765) Mor. 12802; *Faulds v Townsend* (1861) 23 D. 437.
[4] See Gloag & Henderson, *Law of Scotland* (2012), paras 31.12–31.13.
[5] *Oliver & Boyd v Marr Typefounding Co* (1901) 9 S.L.T. 170; *International Banking Corporation v Ferguson, Shaw & Sons*, 1910 S.C. 182.

Jarvis v Manson
1954 S.L.T. (Sh.Ct) 93

Jewellers bought for £3, renovated, polished (at a cost of £1.50), and resold for £10 a five-stone diamond half-hoop ring. The ring, which was worth £30, had been stolen. *Held*: that the jewellers, being in good faith, were liable to the true owner to the extent of their enrichment from the resale (£5.50).

North-West Securities Ltd v Barrhead Coachworks Ltd
1976 S.C. 68

NWS, a finance company, let a car to R on hire purchase. Before completing payment of all instalments due to NWS, R, although not the owner, sold the car to a motor dealer ("BC"), which then sold on to a private purchaser. Under s.27 of the Hire Purchase Act 1964, the private purchaser became owner as a result of this transaction, and NWS was deprived of its rights in the car. *Held*: that BC were only liable to NWS to the extent that they had made a profit on the resale of the car to the private purchaser.

Lastly on enrichment from the use of another's property, there are cases about the *misappropriation of someone else's funds*.

Bennett v Carse
1990 S.L.T. 454

B was negotiating to buy a pub from X. Although the contract was not yet finalised, B agreed to take entry on February 2, 1987, to make certain payments to X for stock and discharge of debts, and to be responsible for payment of rates on the premises; he also installed C as manager of the pub. B then went abroad for two months. On his return, he discovered that X was no longer willing to sell, but only to lease, the pub, and that he had in fact leased it to C. Further, C had paid the rates on the premises by drawing a cheque on B's account. *Held*: that C was enriched by his actions with B's funds, and was therefore liable to reimburse B.

Performance of another's obligation
Another, more complex enrichment situation is where a party ("P") pays or performs to a creditor ("C") the debt or obligation owed to C by a debtor ("D"), without P having the authority of D to do so. If D's obligation to C is discharged by P's action, then D is enriched by the saving in no longer having to pay or perform to C. This enrichment is at P's expense: P thus has an enrichment claim against D.

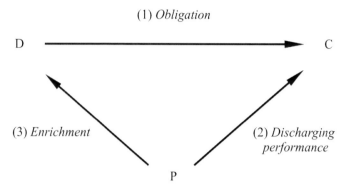

Scots law is, however, still unclear about when unauthorised third party performances discharge D's obligations, although the authorities seem to favour that result.[1] D on his own cannot stop C accepting *payment of money* from P to discharge the debt,[2] and it seems that where P is acting to protect his own legitimate interests—for example, to anticipate and prevent C doing diligence against P for D's debt—he may compel C to accept the payment.[3]

There is more difficulty in the case where *P performs a non-money obligation*—e.g. to build a wall—which D was ready and willing to perform, perhaps at a profit to himself; why should he be deprived of that opportunity by the actions of P as accepted by C, and moreover be subjected to an enrichment claim from P? If P acted despite knowing of D's readiness and willingness to perform, then he may lack a legitimate interest to discharge D's obligation in his own protection, and C will be liable to D for failure to accept his performance; indeed, D may also have a claim against P for inducing C to break a contract. If C enlisted P to get the benefit of a cheaper performance than that offered by D, then P will look to and rely upon C for payment, and it is suggested that his performance can only discharge his own obligations (the issue becomes acute only if C becomes insolvent or otherwise unable to pay his debts before paying P). Moreover, if C pays P for his work, P is not impoverished, even if D is in some sense enriched. P's performance of a non-money obligation may be refused by C if he has a specific interest in personal performance by D (*delectus personae*),[4] and obviously there will be no discharge if C does not accept the performance.

---

[1] For the authorities on this subject, see Gloag and Henderson *The Law of Scotland* (2012), para.3.22; and for further discussion, L.J. Macgregor and N.R. Whitty, "Payment of another's debt, unjustified enrichment and *ad hoc agency*" (2011) 15 *Edinburgh L.R.* 57. The DCFR VIII.-2:107 allows discharge by third party performance if the third party acts with the assent of the debtor or has a legitimate interest in performing and the debtor has failed to perform or it is clear that the debtor will not perform at the time performance is due.

[2] Bankton, *Institute*, 1.24.1 ("he cannot hinder the creditor to take his payment where he can get it").

[3] Bell, *Principles of the Law of Scotland*, 10th edn (1899), para.557.

[4] Bell, *Principles*, para.557. The classic example would be an obligation to paint a portrait.

See for example:

Reid v Lord Ruthven
(1918) 55 S.L.R. 616

Lord R was indebted to a bank. The debts were guaranteed by K, whose own debts were in turn guaranteed by Mr R. On K's death, the bank found that his assets were not enough to cover Lord R's debt. Mr R paid the balance to the bank, which as a result treated Lord R's debt as discharged. Lord R was therefore enriched because he was no longer liable to pay the bank, i.e. he had made a saving, but at Mr R's expense. Lord R was found liable to pay Mr R the amount of the saving.

Duncan v Motherwell Bridge & Engineering Co Ltd
1952 S.C. 131

D was employed by M to work for a period in Kuwait, the contract providing that outward and homeward travel fares at the beginning and end of the contract would be paid by M. During the contract period, D went on strike and was repatriated at his own request. Although not obliged to do so, M paid D's return fare. *Held*: that D was enriched by the payment of his fare by M.

Lawrence Building Co v Lanarkshire County Council
1978 S.C. 30

LBC built houses in Lanark. Lanark Town Council ("LTC") had a statutory obligation to construct sewers that would connect the houses to the existing system of public sewers. The work of building the sewers was in fact done by LBC, who expected LTC to pay for it. Local government re-organisation meant that LTC was replaced by LCC, which refused to pay for the sewers. LCC was found to be enriched by the saving which it had made, in not having to construct the sewers despite the statutory obligation to do so; thus LBC had a relevant claim.

Note that this last case involves performance of another's non-money obligation, but does not raise the issues about that topic discussed in the text above, because, the obligation being statutory, the creditor is the public paying local government taxes in Lanarkshire, and the debtor ("LCC") is not a profit-making organisation. Contrast this decision with the very similar, earlier case of *Varney (Scotland) Ltd v Burgh of Lanark*,[1] where recompense was not allowed; the parties had been in dispute about liability to construct the sewers, and the contractors should have brought an action against the council for implement of its statutory duty, rather than proceeding to build the sewers.

---

[1] *Varney (Scotland) Ltd v Burgh of Lanark*, 1974 S.C. 245.

ENRICHMENT GENERALLY:
TRANSFER, IMPOSITION AND TAKING

All these examples of enrichment help us to understand why different remedies may be required in enrichment law. In some cases, restoration of the specific thing will be appropriate: money, for example (although, since money is fungible, the money repaid need not be exactly the same notes and coins that were originally received), or goods. But improvements, services, and use of property can never be restored; instead they will have to be valued and paid for. Similarly, with cases where the recipient of goods has consumed them, passed them on to others, or otherwise created a situation where they cannot be returned as they were received. Where a debt or obligation has been paid or performed by a third party, it too cannot be returned as such, although at least the amount of the money debt discharged can be precisely fixed.[1]

A very important distinction lies in the way enrichment comes about, and is caught in the phrase "receipt or acquisition" used at the beginning of this chapter (see p.8). A person may be enriched in a relatively passive way, by merely receiving and accepting the enrichment from someone else: that is, another person acts to make the enrichment, for example, by paying over a sum of money or handing over goods. The enrichment is *transferred to* the enriched person by someone else. Again, in some other cases, the enrichment is *imposed upon* the enriched person by someone else, e.g. by carrying out improvements to another person's property or paying someone else's debt. In both cases the enriched party receives enrichment in a relatively passive way: the difference between the transfer and the imposition cases is that there is no need for the beneficiary to cooperate or consent in the latter; he has the enrichment regardless. This, of course, gives rise to issues about how to distinguish between the cases where such imposed enrichment must be paid for, and when the law should rather protect the recipient from unsought interventions in their affairs (see further below, pp.43–45).

On the other hand, a person may take active steps to acquire an enrichment, typically by making use in some way of another person's property, rights, or money. The enrichment is *taken*, or achieved by way of *encroachment upon, interference with, or invasion of, another's rights.* Henceforth these actions will be generically described as "takings", although they encompass a wide range of actions by the enriched person. Improving someone else's property or paying their debts is not such taking to acquire enrichment, because the active person (the improver or the payer) confers, rather than gains, enrichment in these situations. Note however, that the taking must be unauthorised, so that if the owner of the right consents to it, no enrichment claim will arise on this ground. As the discussion of property use cases above showed, however, there are examples in Scots law of enrichment being found to arise from use of

---

property to which the owner consented, but it was apparent from the circumstances that this was not done gratuitously. Such cases may often be ones of contract rather than enrichment;[1] but insofar as they are to be located within enrichment law, they are best seen as transfer rather than taking cases.

In summary then:

- **Enrichment by TRANSFER**—impoverished person ("P") delivers enriching subject-matter (money, corporeal property) to enriched person ("D"); D consents by receiving rather than refusing transfer.
- **IMPOSED enrichment**—P enriches D by an act other than transfer of an enriching subject-matter and without D's consent or authorisation to do so (e.g. improves D's property, pays D's debt to a third party).
- **Enrichment by TAKING (encroachment upon/interference with/invasion of another's property/rights)**—D enriches himself by way of use of P's property or other rights without P's consent or authorisation.

The distinctions between enrichment by transfer, imposition and taking help to tell us at whose expense the enrichment is acquired—the transferor, the imposer, or the owner/holder of the right taken, respectively—but its greatest importance is in determining which factors should be used to establish whether the enrichment is unjustified and should be restored or paid for. See further below, Ch.4.

The structure is one with origins in the German law of unjustified enrichment, and is also found in use now in Israel, as well as being proposed for South African law by Professors Daniel Visser and Jacques du Plessis (partly influenced by the Scottish experience).[2] It also corresponds with the groupings of enrichment cases in the DCFR, which looks like this:

"An enrichment is attributable to another's disadvantage … where
(a) an asset of that other is transferred to the enriched person by that other;
(b) a service is rendered or work is done for the enriched person by that other;
(c) the enriched person uses that other's asset, especially where the enriched person infringes the disadvantaged peron's rights or legally protected interests;
(d) an asset of the enriched person is improved by that other; or
(e) the enriched person is discharged from a liability by that other."[3]

[1] See, e.g. *Shetland Islands Council v BP Petroleum Development Ltd*, 1990 S.L.T. 82 (above, p.12).
[2] On German enrichment law, see R. Zimmermann and J. du Plessis, "Basic features of the German law of unjustified enrichment" [1994] 2 R.L.R. 14; for Israel see H.L. MacQueen, "Unjustified enrichment in mixed legal systems" [2005] 13 R.L.R. 21 at pp. 22–23; and for South Africa see D. Visser, *Unjustified Enrichment* (2008) and J. du Plessis, *The South African Law of Unjustified Enrichment* (2012).
[3] DCFR VII.-4:101.

In this list (a) and (b) correspond to our "transfer" category, the split distinguishing the cases where an asset is transferred from those where an intangible benefit is conferred. Our "taking" corresponds with the DCFR's (c), while "imposition" is covered by (d) and (e), which distinguish between the cases of improvements and performance of another's obligation.

FURTHER READING

The essential text is Robin Evans-Jones, ***Unjustified Enrichment Volume 1: Enrichment by Deliberate Conferral: Condictio*** (2014). The volume deals in detail with what this book calls "enrichment by transfer". Volume 2, expected to appear later in 2013, will cover "enrichment by taking and by imposition".

3. AT ANOTHER'S EXPENSE
(LOSS AND CAUSATION)

LOSS

To be returnable, an enrichment must be gained at the expense of another; that is to say, usually another person must have suffered a loss, a diminution or reduction in wealth which is in some sense the result or consequence of the other's enrichment.[1] Again the DCFR provides a convenient summation of what it refers to as "disadvantage" rather than loss, paralleling its definition of enrichment (above, p.8):

> "A person is disadvantaged by:
> • a decrease in assets or an increase in liabilities;
> • rendering a service or doing work;
> • another's use of that person's assets."[2]

In transfer cases, identifying loss is usually a relatively straightforward matter, because the transferee's gain has a mirror image in the transferor's loss of the amount transferred. Where enrichment arises from takings, the loss can usually be seen as the inability of that other to make, or bargain for the, use of its own property or rights. In cases of imposed enrichment, such as improvements to another's property or payment of another's debt, loss can be readily identified in the cost of carrying out the improvements or making the payment. But in improvement cases, the loss may be much greater than the enrichment on the other side, as where expensive works are carried out, but lead to a much lesser increase in the value of the property concerned. So, it is important to emphasise that the role of the loss in enrichment cases is primarily to help in identifying those cases where there is a right to recover at all, and who has that right. Thereafter, the focus is on the enrichment: the law is concerned to reverse enrichments rather than to compensate for loss.[3] Equally, though, a small expenditure on improvements may result in a much larger increase in the value of the

---

[1] See further, pp.25, 47–50 below, however, for cases where "at the expense of" is not necessarily equiparated with a direct economic loss to the pursuer.

[2] DCFR VII.-3:102(1).

[3] See the criticism of *Smiths Gore v Reilly*, 2003 S.L.T. (Sh.Ct.) 15 on this point, below, p.71–72.

property,[1] and here, it would seem, the amount of the loss is the limit of what can be recovered in any enrichment action; pursuers are not to make a profit out of enrichment claims.[2]

NO LOSS: INCIDENTAL BENEFITS

The enrichment must generally not be an incidental or chance outcome of the pursuer's expenditure. If somebody does something for his own benefit, which also incidentally confers a benefit on another, the former probably suffers no relevant loss; the latter's benefit did not cause him any extra expenditure. As noted in *Exchange Telegraph Co Ltd v Giulianotti*,[3] a case of unauthorised use of a subscription sports news service, "the fact that the defender by obtaining the news service from other subscribers incidentally benefited did not involve the pursuers in any extra expenditure".[4] A famous illustration was given by Lord President Dunedin in *Edinburgh and District Tramways Co Ltd v Courtenay*:

> "One man heats his house, and his neighbour gets a great deal of benefit. It is absurd to suppose that the person who has heated his house can go to his neighbour and say, 'Give me so much for my coal bill, because you have been warmed by what I have done, and I did not intend to give you a present of it.'"

Edinburgh and District Tramways Co Ltd v Courtenay
1909 S.C. 99

EDT ran trams in Edinburgh. C contracted with EDT to provide fittings on the trams, from which boards would be hung to carry advertisements. EDT acquired new trams which already had boards attached, to improve safety and "decency" (i.e. not expose the legs of the passengers, female ones especially, to onlookers). C thus no longer had to incur the expense of providing the fittings, but continued to charge EDT the same rate for its services. EDT argued that C, by making a saving in this way, was enriched. It was held that C was only incidentally benefited by expenditure which EDT had engaged upon with their own purposes—safety, decency, attraction of passengers—in mind, and that no claim lay.

---

[1] See the South African case of *Nortje en 'n Ander v Pool* 1966 (3) S.A. 96 (A.) (above, p.11), where expenditure of R800 enhanced the value of the defendant's property by R15,000. This type of situation has led to the comment that the easiest way to ruin somebody is to enrich him.

[2] Hume, *Lectures*, Vol.3, pp.166–167.

[3] *Exchange Telegraph Co Ltd v Giulianotti*, 1959 S.C. 19.

[4] *Exchange Telegraph Co Ltd v Giulianotti*, 1959 S.C. 19 at 26, per Lord Guest.

[5] *Edinburgh and District Tramways Co Ltd v Courtenay*, 1909 S.C. 99.

[6] *Edinburgh and District Tramways Co Ltd v Courtenay*, 1909 S.C. 99 at 105.

SELFISH OR MIXED MOTIVES

However, it cannot be said that the mere fact that the pursuer carried out expenditure with a view only of his own interests always precludes recovery altogether. Thus, for example, if I improve land in the honest but mistaken belief that it is mine, or if I perform another's obligations to protect my own interests, I am acting for my own benefit; but this will not prevent me recovering for the enrichment of the true owner.[1] Similarly, recovery has been allowed in cases of mixed motives, where the pursuer acted partly in her own interest, partly in that of the defender.[2] The purpose of the expenditure must therefore be seen as merely a factor which can—but need not—be relevant in considering whether or not resultant enrichment is at the expense of the pursuer. After all, if the expenditure was intended to benefit the defender, that may point as much to gift as to unjustified enrichment. As the cases of improving another's property or paying another's debt show, a more important factor than purpose is likely to be the directness with which the enrichment is created for the defender by the pursuer's activities. This also holds good for the takings cases, where the defender enriches himself by using the pursuer's property specifically.[3]

INDIRECT ENRICHMENT

A difficult group of cases is concerned with what is known as "indirect enrichment", where three or more parties are involved in what is sometimes called an enrichment "chain" or "triangle" or "constellation". The situation is one where A has conferred a benefit upon C as a result of another transaction (often a contract) between A and B. In general A will not be allowed to claim against C in this situation.

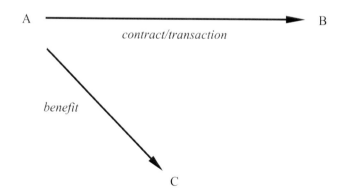

[1] See, e.g. *Newton v Newton*, 1925 S.C. 715; *Lawrence Building Co v Lanarkshire County Council*, 1978 S.C. 30.
[2] See, e.g. *Fernie v Robertson* (1871) 9 M. 437, below, p.74.
[3] See the cases listed above, pp.11–13.

So, for example, if A is a building sub-contractor who performs work under the sub-contract with B, thereby benefiting C, the building owner, but A is not paid by B because B has become insolvent, A does not have an enrichment claim against C for the work done.[1] This is because the law holds that A in entering the sub-contract relied only on the credit of the other contracting party and, therefore, bears the risk of B's insolvency and is limited to its contractual claim against B. The same result occurs in what are often known as the "garage repair" cases, where A is the repairer of C's damaged car, but is actually performing the repair under contract with C's insurers, B. If B becomes insolvent before paying A, the latter has no claim against C for the enrichment arising from the repair.[2]

However, in some cases of indirect enrichment recovery will be allowed, because the policy factors in favour of recovery outweigh those against it described above.[3]

M&I Instrument Engineers Ltd v Varsada and Beattie
1991 S.L.T. 106

V defrauded M&I of £50,000 cash by falsely telling the company's directors that he represented a Saudi sheikh setting up a catering consultancy, and persuading them to invest in this new business. The next day V used £41,240 of the cash to buy a house at Shawhead, Dumfries, in the name of his mistress B.

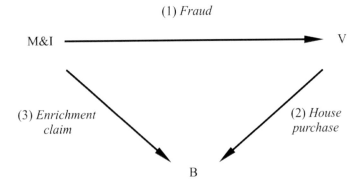

(1) *Fraud*

(3) *Enrichment claim*

(2) *House purchase*

---

[1] See for this example *JB Mackenzie (Edinburgh) Ltd v Lord Advocate*, 1972 S.C. 231 (where the unsuccessful claim was made in delict).

[2] *Kirklands Garage (Kinross) Ltd v Clark*, 1967 S.L.T. (Sh.Ct) 60; *Express Coach Finishers v Caulfield*, 1968 S.L.T. (Sh.Ct) 11. Contrast the South African cases of *ABSA Bank v Stander* 1998 (1) S.A. 939 (C.) and *McCarthy Retail Ltd v Shortdistance Carriers CC* 2001 (3) S.A. 482 (S.C.A.). See further D.P. Visser and S. Miller, "Between principle and policy: indirect enrichment in subcontractor and 'garage repair' cases" (2000) 117 *South African L.J.* 594.

[3] In addition to the cases described below, see *Extruded Welding Wire (Sales) Ltd v McLachlan & Brown*, 1986 S.L.T. 314; *McGraddie v McGraddie* [2012] CSIH 23 (although here equity was said to be the prime consideration rather than policy).

V was arrested, convicted and jailed for the fraud, but M&I were unable to recover the £50,000 from him. On release from prison, V lived with B in the Shawhead house. M&I sought restitution of £41,240 from B. *Held*: that although B was only an indirect beneficiary of the fraudulent transaction between M&I and V, no person should be entitled to profit from the fraud of another, and she should repay the sum sought to M&I.

Mercedes-Benz Finance Ltd v Clydesdale Bank Plc
1997 S.L.T. 905

MB supplied cars to GH for sale by the latter. GH paid the proceeds of such sales to its bank, CB, and MB claimed the payments due to it for the cars by way of a direct debit on GH's account with CB.

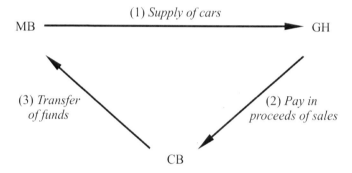

GH was heavily indebted to CB in other respects, and for that reason CB decided not to make a payment under the arrangements with MB. GH then became insolvent. *Held*: with hesitation, that MB had a relevant enrichment claim against CB because the bank knew about the purpose of GH's payments to it, which would not have been made but for the agreement of the bank that they would be applied for the benefit of MB.

It seems impossible to lay down general rules as to when an indirect enrichment claim will or will not be allowed, although typical situations can be identified and may yield up rules for those situations. While the main trend of Scottish authority is against recovery of indirect enrichment,[1] there is no absolute bar; and the modern recognition of the general principle against unjustified enrichment may mean that some of the existing cases of non-recovery—e.g. the "garage repair" cases—will come under review in future. As has been said by one author:

---

[1] See also recently *GW Tait & Sons v Taylor*, 2002 S.L.T. 1285.

"[T]hree-party situations are just too varied and complex for simple, hard-and-fast rules to be able to provide adequately for their solution … the best we can do in three-party situations is to lay down the general pattern along which a solution should proceed."[1]

That general pattern is to be found in the conventional analysis of enrichment at the expense of another which is not justified, although past authorities may be grouped to give us some indicators of likely outcomes in some typical situations such as the subcontractor and garage repair cases mentioned above (p.22).

Gouws v Jester Pools
1968 (3) S.A. 563

In this South African case a contractor ("I") entered a contract to build a swimming pool for T on land which I understood to belong to T. In fact E was the owner of the land. I built the swimming pool and sought payment from T. But T disappeared without paying, and it emerged that E was the true owner of the land and therefore, by the doctrine of accession, of the pool. Could I recover the value of the pool from E? The South African court thought not; I had relied only on T to be paid. This would seem also to cover the case where T did not pay because he became insolvent. Perhaps the answer would have been different if E, after discovering the existence of the pool, had sold the land at a higher price than it would have commanded without the pool.

Renfrewshire Council v McGinlay
2001 S.L.T. (Sh.Ct.) 79

R leased a shop to J. J ceased to trade and handed the shop over to M, who occupied it without a lease for three years. R, having discovered the situation and having failed to negotiate a lease with M, sought recompense for the latter's use of the property. The action failed, on the basis that R should have sued J under the contract of lease first, under which he would get the three years' rent or the equivalent in damages; there was accordingly a risk of double recovery by R if the action against M was allowed. However, it seems clear that M was enriched and J was probably insolvent or not otherwise worth suing; should R have to accept the risk, not only of such insolvency, but also that its co-contractor would wrongfully allow another to occupy the subject-matter of the contract?

---

[1] D.P. Visser, "Searches for silver bullets: enrichment in three-party situations", in D. Johnston and R. Zimmermann (eds) *Unjustified Enrichment: Key Issues in Comparative Perspective* (2002), Ch.9.

ENRICHMENT RECOVERY ALTHOUGH NC

Finally in this section, cases where there is enri
any economic loss to the pursuer require brie
principally (if not exclusively) in the category of t
example, that as an enthusiastic rider I see in a sm
to another, but being left unexercised and in cor
condition. Without the owner's authority, I take t
thereby enhancing its fitness and value. There is no obvious loss to the
owner—indeed there is probably a benefit—but the benefit which I get
from unauthorised rides on the horse is clearly one for which I must pay by
way of an enrichment claim under Scots law.[1] Other cases of this kind
include ones of breach of fiduciary duty, where fiduciaries such as trustees,
agents, partners and company directors are liable to hand over to those to
whom their duties are owed, any gain which they make as a result of
abusing their fiduciary position, even though there may be no
corresponding loss to the fiduciary creditors.

FURTHER READING

See on indirect enrichment, N.R. Whitty, "Indirect enrichment in Scots law"
1994 *Juridical Review* 200 and 239 (2 parts); R. Evans-Jones, *Unjustified
Enrichment: Enrichment by Deliberate Conferral: Condictio* (2003),
Ch.8; Visser, *Unjustified Enrichment* (2008), pp.193–217, and Du Plessis,
South African Law of Unjustified Enrichment (2012), pp. 151–160, 298–
306.

4. UNJUSTIFIED (WHEN ENRICHMENT IS TO BE REVERSED OR PAID FOR)

Before an enrichment can be reversed, or paid for, its retention by the
enriched person has to be unjustified. The general starting point is that
enrichments will remain where they are, unless a reason can be shown for
their reversal. It is, however, helpful to remember, not only those
circumstances where an enrichment will be considered to be unjustified,
but also those where, because the enrichment is justified, the enriched
person will be entitled to retain it. In the language of the modern cases,
enrichment is justified where there is a legal ground for the retention of the
enrichment. The two major examples of such grounds in Scots law are

---

[1] Example adapted from *Watson, Laidlaw & Co Ltd v Pott, Cassels and Williamson*, 1914
S.C. (H.L.) 18 at 31, per Lord Shaw of Dunfermline.

ichment was the result of an unconditional *gift or donation*,
rformance of a *valid and subsisting contract* (see further below,
2).

om this starting point, Scots law could simply say that, unless the
richment is justified by a legal ground such as a valid contract or gift, it
falls to be reversed. That is the approach of some other legal systems (e.g.
Germany). But Scots law has not yet committed itself quite so far. Such an
approach could throw much of the burden of the law upon the enriched
person, who would have to show affirmative reasons why the enrichment
should be kept. Considerations such as protecting possession and the
security of transactions—so that, once carried through, the law will need
weighty reasons to undo them—have pointed in an opposite direction: it is
for the person who wants to reclaim an enrichment to show reasons why
that should be allowed.

This section returns to the distinction, outlined above (pp.16–18),
between different ways in which enrichment can arise: (i) through a *transfer*
by the impoverished person to the enriched one; (ii) through the *imposition*
of an enrichment upon the enriched person by the activity of the
impoverished one; and (iii) through the *taking* of an enrichment by the
enriched person by way of use of, or interference with, the property or
rights of the impoverished one. This allows differences in the way these
types of enrichment are treated in the law to be made clear.

TRANSFERS

We begin with the situation where enrichment arises through transfer of an
asset, such as money or goods, from the impoverished to the enriched
person. As Lord President Rodger said in *Shilliday v Smith*,[1] the cases where
recovery has been allowed can be put into groups, or categories, which
often correspond with the typology of the Roman law *condictiones*.

The approach in this section follows the model proposed in *Shilliday*,
taking the *condictiones* as the basis for identifying when enrichments are
unjustified. But it is important to remember that here the *condictiones* fall
to be treated in their modern or Scots law guise; that some of the
condictiones found in Roman law have not really been much discussed in
Scots law and are, therefore, not treated in any detail or touched upon at all
here; and that the principle against unjustified enrichment means that the
law, now and in its future development, is not confined to the situations
defined by the *condictiones*.

Enrichment by transfer may be reversed in the following situations:

---

[1] See above, p.4.

Condictio indebiti

"*Condictio indebiti*" means "action for the recovery of an undue (*indebitum*) transfer". The transfer falls to be reversed, because it was not legally due to be made in the first place. But the law has restricted the breadth of this concept because, taken literally, it would mean, e.g., that all gifts were reversible enrichments of the donee, which cannot be right. Instead the donee can retain the gift because gift, or donation, is a recognised legal ground for this (see below, pp.62–63). The typical *condictio indebiti* case in Scots law is where the transferor has made the undue transfer in question as the result of an error that it *was* due by the transferor, because of some legal obligation owed to the transferee/recipient. It is often said that such error is an essential element in making a transfer undue and so reversible.

The courts have taken a reasonably wide approach to what may be an error of this type, although they have not gone so far as to say that any error which causes a transfer to be made permits a claim for its recovery. Thus, if A transfers money or goods to B, meaning to pay or transfer to C, or supplies to B more than he owes to B, the latter is liable to restore the money or goods to A, because A was in error as to his liability towards B. The error may be in *fact* (e.g. the identity of the person to whom A is making the transfer, the quantity due to be transferred under a contract) or (since an important decision in 1995) *in law* (e.g. the power of a local authority to borrow money under local government legislation). Errors as to states of fact or law should be distinguished from mispredictions as to events in the future, e.g. it is an *error* if I think I am married when I am not, because, for example, my partner is party to an earlier and still undissolved marriage; while it is a *misprediction* if I say today that I am going to marry a person to whom I am engaged and, therefore, make a transfer to that person, who then breaks off the engagement the next day. If mispredictions give rise to any claim for the reversal of enrichment, it is under other heads, such as the *condictio causa data causa non secuta* (see further below, pp.32–37).

The 1995 decision of the Scottish courts that error in law might be a basis for the *condictio indebiti* had a significant effect on *Kleinwort Benson v Lincoln City Council*, the English House of Lords decision in 1998 to over-rule the previous view that mistake in law did not ground an action for restitution. But this led the House to discuss the conundrum arising where

---

[1] The approach of the English courts: see *Barclays Bank v Simms* [1980] Q.B. 677.

[2] See *Morgan Guaranty Co of New York v Lothian Regional Council*, 1995 S.C. 151.

[3] *Kleinwort Benson v Lincoln City Council* [1999] 2 A.C. 349. Note especially, from a Scottish point of view, the speech of Lord Hope of Craighead. A further English case in which the Government's mistake of law did not enable it to recover over-payments made to social security claimants because the relevant statutory remedy precluded use of the common law is *R. (on the application of Child Poverty Application Group) v Secretary of State for Work and Pensions* [2011] 2 A.C. 11 (note that Lord Rodger's concurrence in this unanimous decision was made "with some hesitation" (at 33)).

the error of law is the result of a judicial decision post-dating the payment in question. If that decision is merely declaratory, so that previous understandings of the law were wrong (the view of the majority in the House of Lords), then the payment was indeed made under mistake; but if the decision *changes* the law (the minority view), then there was no mistake at the time of payment, but only a misprediction as to the law. This debate may suggest that mistake is not the best conceptual way of tackling the problem. A better overall analysis may be the absence of a legal ground for retaining the payment, subject to a defence that the payer knew that it was not liable to pay, a view which has appealed to the House of Lords for English law.[1]

Returning for the moment to Scots law, *knowledge* that a transfer is not due precludes the *condictio indebiti*. The party who knows that a transfer is not due is, obviously, not labouring under any error on the matter. Error should probably also be distinguished from *doubt* as to whether or not a transfer is due; although doubt excludes knowledge that the transfer is due, it also does not manifest belief that the transfer is due, the basic requirement for recovery under the principle of the *condictio indebiti*.[2]

It is possible, but not necessary, for the error to be shared by the transferee; where the transferee also erroneously thought the transfer was due, the case for restoration is however strengthened.[3] The error may arise from the transferee's misrepresentation;[4] but fraud, it has been said, is not an error for the purposes of the *condictio indebiti*.[5] The transferor's error need not be excusable, although that may be a factor to be weighed in considering the overall equities of a given case (see further below, pp.51–52): that is, if an error is excusable, that favours restoration to the pursuer, while if it is inexcusable, denial of recovery is more likely.[6]

---

[1] See *Deutsche Morgan Grenfell v Inland Revenue Commissioners* [2007] 1 A.C. 558 (summarised below, p.40), supporting without definitively committing to the approach advocated in P. Birks, *Unjust Enrichment* (2005); and S. Meier and R. Zimmermann, (1999) 115 L.Q.R. 556.

[2] See *Balfour v Smith & Logan* (1877) 4 R. 454; J. du Plessis and H. E. Wicke, 1993 S.L.T. (News) 303; Scot. Law Com. DP No.99 (1996), para.4.27; *Kleinwort Benson v Lincoln City Council* (1999) 2 A.C. at 410, per Lord Hope of Craighead; *Deutsche Morgan* (above), paras 20–30 (Lord Hoffmann).

[3] *Hamilton v Western Bank* (1861) 23 D. 1033.

[4] *Balfour v Smith & Logan* (1877) 4 R. 454.

[5] *GM Scott (Willowbank Cooperage) Ltd v York Trailer Co Ltd*, 1969 S.L.T. 87 at 88, per Lord President Clyde. On appeal, the pursuer was allowed to amend his averments from fraud to error (1970 S.L.T. 15).

[6] See further H. Scott, "The requirement of excusable mistake in the context of the *condictio indebiti*: Scottish and South African law compared" (2007) 124 *South African L.J.* 827.

Credit Lyonnais v George Stevenson & Co. Ltd
(1901) 9 S.L.T. 93
(paying the wrong person)

CL, a bank in Paris, remitted certain moneys to the account of GS, merchants in Dundee. This was in error, CL having intended to pay a company of a similar name in Glasgow. The error was discovered 11 months later. GS argued that they had received the money in good faith, believing the money to have been transferred to them through CL by their Paris agent, and had made use of the money on that basis. *Held*: that GS were liable to repay CL, having been negligent in the way they dealt with the payment when it arrived, and not having really altered their position with regard to it since.

Bank of New York v North British Steel Group
1992 S.L.T. 613
(paying the wrong person)

BNY were instructed by customer A to transfer money to another bank to the account of B, but, as the result of a slip entering the account numbers on a computer, erroneously transferred it to the account of NBSG. NBSG were already owed money by A and, when BNY claimed repayment, remitted only the balance beyond the debt they claimed from A. Held: that for BNY to recover they would have to show how they had come to make the error, and its excusability would be a factor for the court to consider before reaching a decision.

British Hydro-Carbon Chemicals and British Transport Commission, Petitioners
1961 S.L.T. 280
(over-payment)

BHCC made payments to BTC under a contract, not realising that under the same contract it was entitled to a rebate on the sums paid. *Held*: that BHCC was entitled to repayment of the amount of the rebate.

Peter Walker & Sons (Edinburgh) Ltd v Leith Glazing Co Ltd
1980 S.L.T. (Sh.Ct) 104
(payment not due under contract)

PWS were contractors under a building contract, and LG were sub-contractors. The PWS chargehand authorised LG to perform extra work under the sub-contract, for which LG were paid by PWS. It was then found that under the sub-contract the charge-hand had had no authority to authorise the work. *Held*: PWS were entitled to recover the payment which had been made under the error that it was contractually due to LG.

Morgan Guaranty v Lothian Regional Council
1995 S.C. 151
(payment made under void contract not due)

For the facts, see above, p.9. Here the error was an error in law (both parties believed, erroneously, that their transaction was valid under local government legislation, and that payments and repayments under the contract were, therefore, legally due).

Example(s) of non-liability errors:

(1)   A bank, in the exercise of its mandate, pays its customer's creditor in the erroneous belief that cheques previously paid into the customer's account represented cleared funds sufficient to cover the transfer. Here the bank's error is not about its liability to make payment, but about whether funds are available meet the liability. The bank should not be able to recover from the customer's creditor (although it may have an action against its customer if the latter's debt is now discharged).[1]

(2)   *Scanlon v Scanlon*, 1990 G.W.D. 12–598: W paid instalments towards the purchase of a car under a hire purchase agreement in which her male partner ("M") was purchaser. She knew that she was not liable under the contract, but mistakenly believed that the car would be jointly owned by her and M. *Held*: that the error, not being as to liability, did not support recovery of the payments from the seller by W.[2]

(3)   *GM Scott (Willowbank Cooperage) Ltd v York Trailer Co Ltd*, 1970 S.L.T. 15: GMS ordered a York trailer from the local representative (Nichol) of YTC. N advised that he could acquire a trailer from a local garage and requested GMS to give him a cheque made out to that garage to enable him to pay them. N used the cheque to pay his own debt to the garage. GMS cancelled the order for the trailer and obtained one from another source; they then claimed repayment of the value of the cheque from YTC (as N's employers) and the garage under the *condictio indebiti*. A proof before answer was allowed. Per Lord Walker (dissenting, at p.21):

---

[1]   Based on the English case of *Lloyds Bank Plc v Independent Insurance Co Ltd* [2000] Q.B. 110.

[2]   Although she did succeed against M, presumably on the basis of *causa data causa non secuta* (see further below, pp.32–37).

"Since the reclaiming motion was enrolled, the pursue.
allowed to amend to the effect that they made the paym.
second defenders in the mistaken belief that they would rec.
exchange a trailer supplied by the second defenders. That is no.
think, an averment they were presently due that sum to the secona
defenders. It is no doubt true that they drew the cheque in favour of
the second defenders but their averment is that they did so at the
request of Nichol in order that he might in future obtain a trailer from
them. That is a different thing from a mistaken belief that they had
contracted to purchase a trailer from the second defenders and so were
liable to pay the price. In order to found a *conditio indebiti* it is, I
think, essential that the mistake should be in believing a debt to be due
when in truth it is not."

Condictio ob turpem vel injustam causam

The *condictio ob turpem vel injustam causam* was received in Scots law,[1]
and enabled the recovery of a transfer made for an illegal or immoral
purpose. Recovery was however not allowed where the parties to the
transfer were equally responsible for the illegality; then the position of the
possessor was stronger (*in pari delicto potior est conditio possidentis*). This
allowed a relatively flexible evaluation of whether or not there should be
recovery. The question of whether a transfer of value was illegal was
distinct from the one whether any underlying contract was void or
unenforceable as a result of the illegality.

Cuthbertson v Lowes
(1870) 8 M. 1073

Statute declared void contracts of sale using customary rather than
Imperial weights and measures, but the court held that the purchaser
in a bargain for the sale of potatoes by the "Scotch acre", while not
liable for the contract price, was nonetheless bound to account for the
value of the potatoes he had acquired. The statute did not make the
transfer of potatoes for value unlawful.

In the modern development of the law, however, the presence of illegality
in a transfer has tended to be seen, not as a possible ground of, but as a
near absolute barrier to recovery.[2]

---

[1] See Stair, *Institutions of the Law of Scotland*, 6th edn (1981), para.1.7.8; Bankton, *Institute*,
1.8.22.
[2] For another example of non-recovery for illegality see *Barr v Crawford*, 1983 S.L.T. 481.
Slightly greater flexibility of approach is apparent in *Dowling & Rutter v Abacus Frozen
Foods Ltd*, 2002 S.L.T. 491; and *Malik v Ali*, 2004 S.L.T. 1280.

mieson v Watt's Trustee
1950 S.C. 265

atute a licence was required could not be made
for payment under the contract, which was void
gality, or in enrichment law, when it had been
essary licence having been obtained. To allow
subvert the policy underlying the legislation.

The law in this area is now unsatisfactory and inflexible, and reform seems
necessary to deal more justly with the various situations which can arise.[1]
Louisiana and South Africa both have less rigid regimes,[2] while the DCFR
states that although where a contract is void for illegality a person enriched
thereby is not liable to reverse the enrichment, but only to the extent "that
the reversal would contravene the policy underlying the principle or rule"
infringed by the illegality.[3] This seems a more balanced way of tackling the
issue. It may be that the *condictio* could be subsumed within a broader
concept of the *condictio indebiti*, i.e. one that emphasised undue-ness rather
than liability error.

Condictio causa data causa non secuta

This third ground on which an enrichment by transfer may be reversed
(henceforth "CCDCNS"), can be translated as the action for the recovery
of something transferred for a future purpose which failed to materialise.
The underlying idea is that the transferor made a payment, or other transfer,
on the basis of some anticipated return which is now not going to occur.
Accordingly, the transferee has no legal justification for retaining the
money or other property transferred. The classic case referred to in the
Institutional Writers is the engagement rings given to each other by the
parties to the engagement; if the engagement is broken off and the marriage
does not take place, then the rings must be returned, as the reason for the
gift (the parties' wedding) will not now take place.[4] The same would apply
to wedding presents purchased in advance, which are clearly a conditional
gift.

Many modern cases on the CCDCNS have arisen, not out of
engagements to marry, but from arrangements between men and women
cohabiting and planning, with more or less enthusiasm on each side, to
marry.

---

[1] See L.J. Macgregor, "Illegal contracts and unjustified enrichment" (2000) 4 Edinburgh
L.R. 19.

[2] See H.L. MacQueen and A. Cockrell, "Illegal contracts", in R. Zimmermann, D. Visser
and K. Reid (eds), *Mixed Legal Systems in Comparative Perspective: Property and
Obligations in Scotland and South Africa* (2004); H.L. MacQueen, "Unjustified enrichment,
subsidiarity and contract", in Palmer and Reid, *Mixed Jurisdictions Compared: Private
Law in Louisiana and Scotland* (2009), at 333.

[3] DCFR VII.-6:103. See VII.-7:301–304 for when contracts are illegal.

[4] Stair, *Institutions*, 1.7.7; Bankton, *Institute*, 1.8.21; Erskine, *Institutes of the Law of
Scotland*, 7th edn (1871) 3.1.9, 10.

Shilliday v Smith
1998 S.C. 725

M and W began to live together in M's cottage in 1988, and became engaged in August 1990. They never married. In 1988, M had bought a house in a state of disrepair, and from about 1990 M and W began to improve this property, into which they moved together in 1991. The works were completed by Christmas 1992, when M ejected W from the house. W had spent about £9,600 on the works: approximately £7,000 direct to tradesmen, £1,880 to M to pay for materials and work on the house, and £756 on items for the garden, left behind after her ejection. It was held that W was entitled to repetition of the £1,880 she had paid to M on the basis of CCDCNS; she had made her payments in contemplation of a marriage which did not take place. On the same principle, she was entitled to recompense for what she had expended on tradesmen and other items, the benefit of which was now being enjoyed by M.

Compare:

Grieve v Morrison
1993 S.L.T. 852

G and M decided to live together on the understanding that they would marry when G's first marriage was terminated by divorce. M bought a flat in which the parties lived, and the loan for which was paid by her. Later this flat was sold and another purchased, on the same basis as the first; G contributed work and money to the cost of renovations. The parties fixed their wedding for August 1984, and in October 1983 jointly purchased another flat, with a joint loan and the free proceeds of the sale of M's previous flat. G had always had considerable, but unexpressed, reservations about the wedding, but he only told M about this one month after they had moved into the new flat; he then left the property. G subsequently brought an action for division or sale of the flat. M argued on the basis of the CCDCNS that she was entitled to G's share of the property (rather than to any part of the free proceeds of the sale of the property), because the arrangements had been made on the basis that the parties would marry. The court held that M had no such claim to G's share and that, for her to have any claim even to the proceeds of the sale of the property beyond her half, she would have to show: (i) that the arrangements had been made on the basis of a mutually agreed understanding that was either express, or to be implied, from the circumstances; and (ii) that she had made a contribution to the pursuer's share of the price of the property.

While *Grieve* seems to be correctly decided, the comments about the need to show an express, or implied, mutually agreed understanding—that the transfer to be reversed was made on the basis of some future event occurring—must be read in the light of dicta of Lord President Rodger in *Shilliday*, explaining that it was not necessary for the transfer to be conditional, in any technical sense, upon the happening of the future event:

> "The important thing to notice is that ... the duty to restore is said to be based not on agreement (paction), but on a natural ground, i.e. it is a duty imposed by law. This is a useful reminder that...the basis of liability to reverse unjust enrichment is not contractual but rests on this separate duty imposed by law. Counsel was therefore correct to argue that there was no need for the pursuer to point to any kind of contract between the parties under which the pursuer paid the various sums on condition that they married."[1]

The first question in CCDCNS cases is therefore—what was the cause of, or reason for, the transaction from the point of view of the transferor?—not whether both parties had agreed, or understood, that the transfer would fall to be reversed if a particular future event did not occur. But in *Shilliday* it also mattered that "the defender knew that the pursuer was expending money on his house which the parties had agreed would be their matrimonial home, and ... all that she did was done in contemplation of the parties' marriage". Hence, although one must look at the cause of, or reason for, the transaction from the point of view of the transferor, that is not enough. The pursuer must also prove that the defender had knowledge of this purpose or cause.

The DCFR provides a formula which may be worth considering for Scots law:

> "An enrichment is also unjustified if:

(a)   the disadvantaged person conferred it:
        (i) for a purpose which is not achieved; or
        (ii) with an expectation which is not realised;
(b)   the enriched person knew of, or could reasonably be expected to know of, the purpose or expectation; and
(c)   the enriched person accepted or could reasonably be assumed to have accepted that the enrichment must be reversed in such circumstances."

---

[1] *Shilliday v Smith*, 1998 S.C. 725 at 730.
[2] DCFR VII.-2:101(4).

With such a non-contractual understanding of the meaning of *causa*, some doubt may be cast upon the analysis in sheriff court cases where the CCDCNS was applied to reverse transfers between cohabiting couples who had no plans (or no firm ones) to marry.[1] The evidence was rather that the transfers were made on the basis that the parties would continue to live together and care for each other. So when the relationship broke down and the parties separated, it was not so much a case of *causa non secuta* as of *causa finita*—that is, the basis of the transfer was an existing rather than a future state of affairs, and that state of affairs had now come to an end. If so, then there is another, more appropriate condictio—*ob causam finitam*—which should have been referred to in this situation, rather than the CCDCNS (see above, p.2). The *condictio ob causam finitam* is mentioned by the Institutional Writers but has not been much used in decided cases.[2]

On the other hand, the CCDCNS seems to be properly applied in other cases allowing recovery of: (i) a share of the purchase price of a property to be jointly owned and lived in by the parties, but where the defender neither contributed to the price not cohabited there with the pursuer;[3] and (ii) a contribution to the costs of building an extension to the defender's house in which the pursuer was to live but this was prevented by the defender's sale of the whole property after the extension was completed.[4]

If *Shilliday* shows that the purpose (*causa*) of the transfer need not be contractual in nature, or based upon the express or implied agreement of transferor and transferee,[5] a number of other CCDCNS cases do nonetheless have a contractual dimension. This may be a special feature of the way in which Scots law has developed the original Roman law idea of the CCDCNS, which applied only to informal agreements or mutually agreed understandings outside contract. Modern Scots law is however far more generous than Roman law in its recognition of what may be a contract.

The starting point for the modern development of Scots law on contractual situations and the CCDCNS was *Watson v Shankland*,[6] a shipping case about recovery of a payment made in advance of freight for the carriage of goods by sea. The ship in question had sunk during its voyage, without fault on the part of the master and crew. Lord President Inglis, holding the advance to be recoverable, said:

---

[1] *Satchwell v McIntosh*, 2006 S.L.T. (Sh. Ct.) 117, criticised by R. Evans-Jones (2007) 11 *Edinburgh L.R.* 105. See also *Moggach v Milne*, 2005 G.W.D. 8–107 (Sheriff Principal Sir Stephen Young Q.C., Elgin). The financial position of cohabitants whose relationship has broken down is also dealt with by statute: Family Law (Scotland) Act 2006, ss.25–28. See Gloag & Henderson, *The Law of Scotland* (2012), para.44.36; also *Harley v Robertson*, 2012 G.W.D. 4–68 Falkirk Sheriff Court, December 9, 2011 (Sheriff C Caldwell).

[2] See, e.g. Craig, *Jus Feudale*, 3.5.23; Stair, *Institutions*, 1.7.7; and further Evans-Jones, *Unjustified Enrichment* (2003), paras 6.06–11.

[3] *McKenzie v Nutter*, 2007 S.L.T. (Sh.Ct.) 17. Cf. *Gibson v Gibson and Gavryluk*, 2010 G.W.D. 4–68.

[4] *Smith v Barclay*, Unreported, Dundee Sheriff Court, August 29, 2006.

[5] See, as possible examples in illustration of the proposition here advanced, *McCafferty v McCafferty*, 2000 S.C.L.R. 256; and *Harris v Sales' Exrs*, 2003 G.W.D. 7–186.

[6] *Watson v Shankland* (1871) 10 M. 142; affirmed (1873) 11 M. (H.L.) 51.

"There is no rule of the civil law, as adopted into all modern municipal codes and systems, better understood than this—that if money is advanced by one party to a mutual contract, on the condition and stipulation that something shall be afterwards paid or performed by the other party, and the latter party fails in performing his part of the contract, the former is entitled to repayment of his advance, on the ground of failure of consideration. In the Roman system the demand for repayment took the form of a *condictio causa data causa non secuta*, or a *condictio sine causa*, or a *condictio indebiti*, according to the particular circumstances. In our own practice these remedies are represented by the action of restitution and the action of repetition."[1]

This approach, allowing recovery of advance payments after the full performance of contracts was frustrated by supervening events, was taken much further by the House of Lords in the leading case of *Cantiere San Rocco v Clyde Shipbuilding Co.*[2]

Cantiere San Rocco v Clyde Shipbuilding Co Ltd
1923 S.C. (H.L.) 105

In May 1914, Cantiere, an Austrian company, ordered marine engines for a price of £11,550 from Clyde, and made an initial payment of £2,310. In August 1914, before Clyde could do much significant work on the order, war broke out, and the contract was frustrated by the supervening illegality arising from Cantiere now being an enemy alien company. After the war ended in 1918, Cantiere, now an Italian company, successfully sought repayment of the advance payment on the grounds that the performance had not been met by any counter-performance from Clyde. This was held to be an instance of CCDCNS. Lord Dunedin explained:

"[T]he very short point on which, in my view, the whole case turns. Was the £2,310 paid in respect of the signing of the contract? If it were, then it cannot be said that there was a *causa non secuta*. In other words, if the £2,310 had been conditioned to be paid for signing the contract, my opinion would have been different. But it is not so. It is to be paid on signing the contract. It had, indeed, no separate existence. It is only an instalment of the total price which is the consideration for the whole engine. There is no splitting of the consideration."

Recovery was not prevented merely because Cantiere had made its payment as the result of a contractual obligation valid at the time of

---

[1] *Watson v Shankland* (1871) 10 M. 142 at 152.
[2] *Cantiere San Rocco v Clyde Shipbuilding Co*, 1923 S.C. (H.L.) 105.

payment; the payment had not met with the anticipated counter-performance by Clyde (construction of the engines), and now never would be; therefore the payment fell to be returned.

Cantiere extends the Inglis *dictum* in *Watson v Shankland* because the payment in the former case was not an advance, but was rather an instalment of the full price due under the contract. The House of Lords was, however, quite clear that the CCDCNS principle was not limited to advances, but applied to all cases where a contractual performance had not been met by its corresponding counter-performance from the other party. This makes it very important to analyse the relationship between the two sides of the contract in such cases. If the party now seeking to recover its performance has actually received the counter-performance, the CCDCNS will not lie.

Connelly v Simpson
1993 S.C. 391

C paid £16,000 to S for one-third of the shares in S's company, but the parties agreed to defer delivery, enabling C to minimise the value of his estate during his divorce proceedings, which were also under way at this time. Over the next two years, the company did badly: S first issued more shares to raise capital, thereby diluting the value of C's holding, and then put the company into voluntary liquidation. The liquidator offered C £400, the value of his shares now. C claimed his £16,000 back from S under the CCDCNS. His action failed, Lord Brand dissenting. The majority judges differ as to the reasons for the outcome. One was of the view that C had received what he paid for, viz, a right to delivery of shares on demand. Another thought that the CCDCNS applied only in cases of frustration, which this was not, and otherwise could not be used in contract cases. The judges were clearly reluctant to allow C to escape the consequences of what had turned out to be a bad bargain in a market necessarily involving risk. If the case is rightly decided, it is probably on the basis that the purpose of C's payment had been fulfilled, probably at the time he made it, and so S could not be made liable to repay.

It has been suggested that *Cantiere* is not a case of *causa non secuta*, but rather another one for the *condictio ob causam finitam* (i.e. one where an existing state of affairs—here, the contract—provided the reason for the payment but it came to an end).[1] Could such an analysis apply in the *Connelly* case as well? Did C make his payment on the basis that S's company was solvent? It seems likely, however, that the objection to allowing people to escape the consequences of bad bargains would apply to prevent such a wide approach to this *condictio*.

---

[1] See *Parkin v Smuts*, 1978 3 S.A. 55 (T) (Van Reenan J.).

Condictio sine causa

As already mentioned (above, p.2), in Roman law the *condictio ob causam finitam* was an instance of the more general *condictio sine causa*, under which the general principle was that transfers without a legal basis or justification were to be restored. In some sense the *condictio sine causa* was a residual category, picking up cases for restoration not covered by more specific *condictiones*. This explains why enrichment recovery is allowed in some cases where payments or other transfers are made when not due, but without a liability error being the reason the transfer occurs. Here are some examples where recovery has been allowed without there being a liability error:

(1) Compulsion

The Scottish courts have recognised that transfers made under unlawful compulsion from the transferee may give rise to claims for reversal of those transfers.[1] Such transfers will not however be made under errors as to liability; the transferor may well be very clear about not being liable, but nonetheless is compelled to carry the transaction through.

British Oxygen Co v South of Scotland Electricity Board
1959 S.C. (H.L.) 17

> SSEB, which was a statutory monopoly supplier of electricity, supplied BO with electricity at a high voltage. The supply cost less to provide than a low voltage one, but, in breach of the relevant statute, the tariff of charges applied by SSEB did not differentiate properly between high and low voltage customers. So, BO ended up paying too much, but was under no error about it. It protested but was told by SSEB that if it did not pay, its electricity supply would be cut. In claiming recovery of overpayments, BO argued, successfully, that to remain operative it had had no choice but to pay too much, since SSEB was the only available electricity supplier. BO was, therefore, paying under compulsion and could recover.

If error is the only ground for the *condictio indebiti*, it follows that the cases allowing recovery for compulsion must be treated under some other head to be consistent with the approach in *Shilliday*. Candidates amongst the *condictiones* are the *condictio ob turpem vel injustam causam* (action for recovery of a transfer made for an illegal or immoral purpose, above, pp.31–32; i.e. in this case, to relieve the pressure resulting from improper compulsion) and the *condictio sine causa* (i.e. a transfer made subject to unlawful compulsion cannot be upheld because the transferee has no legal ground, that is, no valid indebtedness of the transferor, on which to retain it). If, however, the *condictio indebiti* was not confined to error cases, but

---

[1] See generally J.E. du Plessis, *Compulsion and Restitution* (Stair Society, 2004), Vol. 51.

was applied in cases where, for whatever reason, the transfer was not legally due, without regard to the subjective intention of the transferring party, then the law would certainly be simpler to state, and we would not need to bring in the *condictio sine causa* to deal with compulsion cases.

(2) Payments subject to protests and reservations

A party may pay another while thinking that he is not liable to do so while making clear protests against the payments and reserving legal rights in the matter. What is happening in such cases is that, for various reasons, the party making the payment wishes to sue for recovery, rather than be subjected to an action for payment. Again, if the *condictio indebiti* is restricted to cases of error, some other basis is going to have to be found for recovery. Scots law seems to be to the effect that mere protest is not enough to justify recovery of the payment: the recipient must be made aware of a definite reservation of rights.[1]

Nurdin & Peacock Plc v Ramsden & Co Ltd
(1999) 1 W.L.R. 1249

P paid D despite doubts as to liability to do so, and also assuming, wrongly, that in law he could recover if the liability did not exist. D knew that P paid under reservation of a right to recover. Held: P could recover for mistake of law.

In Scotland, because P's mistake was probably not a liability mistake, he would have had difficulty recovering under the error-based *condictio indebiti*. D's awareness that P was reserving his rights would probably have meant that the *condictio sine causa* was the appropriate basis of any recovery.

(3) Ultra vires demands by public authorities

It may be that, where a payment is made to a public body acting under statutory powers, the mere fact that the legislation does not justify the payment, or the demand for it, suffices for recovery.[2]

Woolwich Building Society v Inland Revenue
[1993] A.C. 70

W made three payments totalling £57 million to the IR in response to a tax demand made under the Income Tax (Building Societies) Regulations 1986. W disputed the validity of the Regulations but made the payments because it feared penalties and adverse publicity

---

[1] W.M. Gloag, *The Law of Contract*, 2nd edn (1929), p.63. For a critique of the English case of *Nurdin* summarised below, see G. Virgo [1999] *Cambridge L.J.* 478; see also above, p.28.

[2] See also *Stonehaven Magistrates v Kincardine County Council*, 1939 S.C. 760; *Haggarty v Scottish TGWU*, 1955 S.C. 109.

if it did not. In subsequent litigation, it was first found that the Regulations were indeed invalid. In a second case the House of Lords held (by a majority of 3:2, with the Scottish Law Lords forming the minority) that W was entitled to restitution of its payments, plus interest running from the dates of payment, since the money had been paid as the result of an ultra vires demand.

From a Scottish point of view, the case is important because W were never under any error as to whether the payment was due; they always thought it was not. If this means that the *conditio indebiti* does not lie in Scotland, the case would have to be dealt with as one for either the *conditio ob turpem vel injustam causam* (W was improperly compelled by an ultra vires demand to pay IR) or the *conditio sine causa* (being ultra vires, IR had no legal justification for retaining the money). But if the *conditio indebiti* was not limited to cases of error, then, since the payments by W were not due to the IR, they would be recoverable on the ground of simply being undue.

The scope of *Woolwich* was considered again by the House of Lords in an English case:

Deutsche Morgan Grenfell v Inland Revenue Commissioners
[2007] 1 A.C. 558

The claim was to recover money paid as tax which turned out not to have been due (as the result of a decision to that effect by the European Court of Justice). DMG claimed restitution either under the rule in *Woolwich* (undue tax payments must be repaid) or for mistake of law (*Kleinwort Benson v Lincoln City Council* (above, p.27)). The IRC said that DMG was out of time under applicable limitation rules. DMG argued that, since it paid by mistake, it could rely on a special limitation-extension rule for mistaken payers (limitation does not run against a party that does not know of its mistake and could not with reasonable diligence have discovered it), whether it was claiming under *Woolwich* or *Kleinwort Benson*. There were three major issues:

(i) did the limitation-extension rule apply only where C relied on mistake as his ground of recovery (*Kleinwort Benson*), or was it available whatever ground of recovery is relied on, provided that mistake is present on the facts?;

(ii) are claimants restricted to *Woolwich* as their ground of recovery where it is available on the facts, or should they be allowed also to rely on any alternative ground which is also available, e.g. mistake or duress?; and

(iii) does English enrichment law require claimants to establish a positive ground for restitution such as mistake, or does it require them only to establish an absence of legal ground for the transfer to the enriched person (here the IRC)?

The House of Lords held for DMG, finding that there was a mistake in law and that the limitation-extension rule applied. But a number of their Lordships were attracted by the absence of legal ground model, with Lord Walker of Gestingthorpe referring approvingly to the model of Scots law in this regard.

A Scottish court, properly advised, might have approached this case on the basis that the Inland Revenue's retention of the payment lacked a legal basis and it therefore fell to be restored. The discussion about mistake or error would not be necessary if the case is one of the *condictio sine causa* because the tax payment lacked any legal basis.[1] The same would apply if the *condictio indebiti* simply looked to see whether or not a payment was legally due, rather than requiring the payer to show that it had made a liability error. One imagines that the Scottish courts would follow the House of Lords in not getting stuck on the issue of whether there is a mistake or merely a misprediction when a settled view of the law upon which transactions such as tax payments have been based is unseated by a subsequent judicial decision.

(4) Bank payments on countermanded cheques

The *condictio sine causa* also seems likely to provide the correct principle with which to deal with a common problem, readily illustrated from cases in other jurisdictions: *the position of a bank which pays on a cheque despite having previously received a countermand from the relevant customer/drawer of the cheque.*[2]

The starting point is that the bank cannot debit the customer's account for the cheque. If the bank is not to suffer loss, it must effect recovery from the cheque payee. Assuming that the payee is enriched,[3] it would seem nevertheless that the *condictio indebiti* is inapt to the situation. Although the bank transferred funds to the payee, it did not do so in satisfaction of any liability it had to the payee, but acted rather in discharge of its obligation to its customer. There was no liability and no liability-error on the part of the bank. However, the payee has no legal ground on which it can retain the cheque proceeds against the bank, and recovery can, therefore, be made under the *condictio sine causa*.

---

[1] Under the Prescription and Limitation (Scotland) Act 1973 s.6 Sch.1 para.1(b), the obligation to restore enrichment becomes enforceable, starting the prescriptive period of five years, when the enrichment occurs. The period does not run during any period when the creditor was induced to refrain from making a relevant claim by its own error *induced by the debtor's words or conduct* unless the creditor could have discovered the error with reasonable diligence. The italicised words, which are not found in the English statute, might have been the big stumbling block to recovery by DMG in Scotland. But it seems reasonably clear that the error stopping the prescription clock does not also have to be part of the ground for recovery under the Scottish rules. See, e.g. *Rowan Timber Supplies (Scotland) Ltd v Scottish Water Business Stream Ltd* [2011] CSIH 26.

[2] See *Barclays Bank v Simms* [1980] 1 Q.B. 677 (England); *Govender v Standard Bank of South Africa* 1984 (4) S.A. 392 (C.); *B & H Engineering v First National Bank of South Africa Ltd* 1995 (2) S.A. 279 (A.).

[3] A conclusion not reached in the *B & H Engineering* case, because the payee's debt to the customer was discharged and he had lost any claim he might have had in that direction; but accepted in *Simms* and *Govender*.

(2) Cheque in favour of

Drawer ⟶ Payee

(1) Obligation to customer

(3) Payment on cheque

Bank

Similar reasoning can be applied to other cases of payments made in error by banks. In *Royal Bank of Scotland v Watt*[1] (see above, p.8, for the full facts), the bank paid out on a fraudulently altered cheque, but could not debit its customer's account because of the fraud (see Bills of Exchange Act 1882, s.64); however, as already stated, there could be recovery from the person to whom payment had been made. Again, since the bank had acted in discharge of an apparent obligation to its customer, its error was not about liability to the recipient of the payment, and the recovery may, therefore, have been based upon the *condictio sine causa*. But in cases where a bank pays out on a cheque with forged endorsement of the payee's signature, the amount can be deducted from its customer's account as a result of the protection provided by s.60 of the Bills of Exchange Act, and the bank needs no enrichment claim against the payee; the impoverished person is rather the bank's customer.[2]

FURTHER READING

On the *condictiones* in Scots law, see Evans-Jones, **Unjustified Enrichment, Enrichment by Deliberate Conferral: Condictio** (2003), Chs 2–6. J.E. du Plessis, **Compulsion and Restitution** (Stair Society, 2004), Vol.51 is an important and helpful analysis, with extensive historical and comparative discussion. Note also D.R. Macdonald, "Mistaken payments in Scots law", 1989 *Juridical Review* 49.

---

[1] *Royal Bank of Scotland v Watt*, 1991 S.C. 48.
[2] See *Alexander Beith Ltd v Allan*, 1961 S.L.T. (Notes) 80. For a case of fraudulent misuse of a charge card account by a third party, and the liability of the card supplier to the account holder see *Duncan v American Express Services Europe Ltd* [2009] CSIH 1; 2009 S.L.T. 112, analysed by R. Evans-Jones [2010] R.L.R 174.

IMPOSITIONS

The *condictio indebiti*, the CCDCNS, and the other *condictiones* generally do not apply to imposed enrichments, such as the unauthorised improvement of another's property or performance of another's obligation. This no doubt goes some way to explaining why such cases were characteristically dealt with under the heading of recompense in the law before the 1990s. It is however possible for improvements to be made as undue transfers—e.g., if I am a contractor carrying out repairs or enhancements under a void contract[1]—or for a purpose that fails—for example, if I improve my cohabitant's house in anticipation of a marriage that in the end does not take place[2]—and for the beneficiary to be liable as a result. Professor Evans-Jones argues that such cases should not be treated under the heading of impositions, although it is conventional to treat them in that manner, but as transfers.[3] Again, if I pay C the amount of D's debt because I mistakenly think that I am bound to do so, the transfer which is undue is that to C, from whom I can recover on the principle of *condictio indebiti*; but there is no claim against D on that footing. If I pay C because I think that he will then treat D's debt as discharged, but he does not and the debt is indeed not discharged, there might be a claim on the basis of CCDCNS; but again that claim is against C rather than D. Any claim I might have against D will have to be laid on some other basis.

If a general basis of recovery for enrichment imposed without authority is sought, is it provided by the general principle of unjustified enrichment? The enriched person—the one whose property has been improved or obligation discharged—has no legal ground for retaining that enrichment. Even though the improvement forms part of the enriched person's property, that is precisely why he can be regarded as enriched, and it provides no reason for allowing that enrichment to be at the improver's expense. However, at least in the cases of *unauthorised improvements to another's property*, this still seems too wide. So, for example, if I was a building contractor, I could use this principle to go around my home town looking for houses in need of repair, carry out the repairs when the owners were away, and then insist on a right to be paid for the enrichment which I had imposed upon them because they had no legal ground to retain it. Scots law has, therefore, created a number of further conditions to be satisfied before an enrichment claim for improvements will be successful.

These are as follows:

- The impoverished person must have been in good faith possession

---

[1] See, e.g. *Rutherglen Magistrates v Cullen* (1773) 2 Pat. 305; and *Middleton v Newton Display Group Ltd*, 1990 G.W.D. 40–2305 (Glasgow Sheriff Court).

[2] *Shilliday v Smith*, 1998 S.C. 725. Another possible example, although not discussed as such in the case itself, is *Corrie v Craig*, 2013 G.W.D. 1–55; see the case note by M. Hogg, 2013 S.L.T. (News) 111.

[3] R. Evans-Jones, "Searching for 'imposed' enrichment in improvements—classifications and general enrichment actions in mixed systems: Scotland and South Africa" (2008) 16 R.L.R. 18.

of the property while carrying out the improvement, that is, without knowledge of his lack of right to have possession; if the possession is in bad faith (that is, with knowledge of the lack of right), there is no recovery except perhaps for necessary repairs and maintenance.[1]

Barbour v Halliday
(1840) 2 D. 1279

H owned land. On going to America, he left the title deeds with his brother ("H2"). H2 gave the deeds to B in security of a debt owed to B by M, and B then "sold" the ground to G, who carried out improvements. G returned the ground to B, who reimbursed him for his expenditure. H returned from America and, as owner, reclaimed the land with its improvements. B sought reimbursement for the improvements, but was denied because, it was held, his possession had been in bad faith.

The impoverished person must usually have worked under *error*, usually that the property being improved belonged to him.[2] It used to be thought that the owner had to have some sort of apparent title to the property as a basis for this error,[3] but since *Newton v Newton*[4] (above, p.10) this has not been essential so long as the error was in good faith. Improvers possessing on a limited title (for example, as tenants under a lease, or occupying as liferenters) cannot recover,[5] unless such a person erroneously believes him or herself to be an owner.[6] In some cases, the improver's error may be that a third party whom he wishes to benefit is, or will become, the owner of, or entitled to, the property.

Duff, Ross & Co v Kippen
(1871) 8 S.L.R. 299

A partner ("A") in a firm ("AB") spent £234 improving its business premises, believing that they belonged to AB. In fact they belonged to someone else, and the other partner in the firm ("B") was merely a tenant under a lease of the premises. *Held*: the owner was liable to reimburse £234 to A.

---

[1] *Barbour v Halliday* (1840) 2 D. 1279, over-ruling Stair, *Institutions*, 1.8.6. The decision is criticised in R. Evans-Jones (2008) 16 R.L.R. 18 at 36. The inability of the bad faith improver to recover may explain the result in *Corrie v Craig*, 2013 G.W.D. 1-55, on which see further the cases note by M. Hogg, 2013 S.L.T. (News) 111.

[2] Note that cases of improvement, in which error was not required, may well be treatable under another branch of the law, e.g. *Lawrence Building Co v Lanarkshire County Council*, 1978 S.C. 30 is a case of performance of another's obligation.

[3] Note that since the replacement of the Sasine with the modern Land Register a recorded title to land is always a complete and valid one, so that it is no longer possible to possess on a colourable but actually defective recorded title.

[4] *Newton v Newton* 1925 S.C. 715. See for further comment on this case R. Evans-Jones (2005) 9 *Edinburgh L.R.* 449 and (2008) 16 R.L.R. 18 at 33, suggesting that the case is one of CCDCNS.

[5] *Wallace v Braid* (1900) 2 F. 754.

[6] *Morrison v Allan* (1886) 13 R. 1156.

McDowel v McDowel
(1906) 14 S.L.T. 125

Captain M granted his wife ("Mrs M") a 99 year lease over property of which he was heir of entail, and then carried out expensive improvements. The captain's intention in all this was to make provision for his wife after his death. When he died, the lease was found to be invalid. Held: that the captain's son, now owner of the property, was bound to reimburse the deceased captain's estate as represented by his executrix (Mrs M).

Insofar as it is a case of imposed enrichment, *Shilliday v Smith*[1] (see above, p.33) illustrates that there may be recovery without error if some other ground making the enrichment unjustified is present—in that case, *causa data causa non secuta*.[2] There are a number of cases where improvers who knew that their titles were limited, defective, or non-existent, have nevertheless been able to recover.[3]

There are still some difficult precedents where the good faith improver did not recover, but which, in the light of *Shilliday v Smith*, might be decided differently today:

Rankin v Wither
(1886) 13 R. 903

H rebuilt W's house at his own expense, W's intention being to leave H the house if he survived her. But W died before she could execute the necessary settlement on H. *Held* that H could not recover for his improvements. The case is confused: H attempted to prove donation, so that he could bring into play the rule that donations between spouses are revocable, but this failed, on the basis that the expenditure was for his own benefit ultimately and made in the knowledge that he had no title.

Error does not seem to play anything like as important a role in cases of enrichment by unauthorised performance of another's obligation, especially where the performance is *payment of money*. The payer can still recover from the debtor even though he paid the creditor deliberately and with full knowledge of all the relevant facts.[4] What matters is whether or not the debt

---

[1] *Shilliday v Smith*, 1998 S.C. 725. The case is also one where, like *Newton v Newton* (above, p.10), the improver had no apparent title to the property improved.

[2] R. Evans-Jones (2005) 9 *Edinburgh L.R.* 449 suggests that *Newton v Newton* (above, p.10) was also such a case.

[3] e.g. *Nelson v Gordon* (1874) 1 R. 1093; *Reedie v Yeaman* (1875) 12 S.L. Rep. 625; *Yellowlees v Alexander* (1882) 9 R. 765. See discussion of these cases in Evans-Jones (2008) 16 R.L.R. 18 at 36–38.

[4] But note that P's knowledge that he does not owe C means that, if the payment does *not* discharge D's debt, P will not be able to use the *condictio indebiti* to recover the money from C (see p.28 above).

is discharged; and if the creditor treats the payment as doing so, as he generally will, then the debtor is liable. He would have had to pay anyway, under the now discharged obligation; the fact that he is having to pay someone else under a new enrichment obligation makes little or no difference to his basic position. So there is no real need, in that case, to add in protections for the debtor against unwanted intervention in his affairs—especially if he can take against the payer those defences which he would have had against the creditor, such as a right of retention in respect of breach of contract by the creditor.

If the obligation was not a money one, however, the position is more difficult, as can be seen from this hypothetical example:

> C and D have a contract under which D is to build a wall for C. The price is £500. The job will cost D £450, so his profit on the contract is £50. P arranges with C that he will build the same wall for £400, leaving himself a profit of £40, and manages to do the job before D is due to start his operation. C refuses to let D start on building the wall, since he no longer needs D to do the work.

If P can now claim from D the latter's saving in not having to build C's wall—£450—then the former's total profit from his wall operation will be £490, while D will be down by £450 and will also not have his profit of £50 from the contract with C. D is, however, only enriched if P has discharged his obligation, and as discussed above at pp.14–16, that may well not be the case. Moreover, if C has paid P, the latter is not impoverished and any enrichment of D is, therefore, not at P's expense. But the picture becomes more difficult if C is insolvent or otherwise unable to pay P. If D's obligation is discharged, he may be able to offset against any claim by P any costs already incurred in preparing to perform to C; in other words, to demonstrate that there is no enrichment at least to that extent. D's rights against C, in respect of the latter's breach of contract, might also be put in the balance as a matter of the overall equities, even if C was insolvent; setting off against P D's claim for damages for breach by C would cover at least the lost profit, and might also extend to wasted expenditure.[1]

The difficulties which can arise from a third party performing another's non-money obligations also explain why the defence of subsidiarity (see below, pp.53–54) is available in cases of this kind. If the now impoverished party had available an alternative remedy to compel the debtor to perform its obligation, the former's self-help in performing itself will not be allowed to give rise to an enrichment claim against the debtor.

FURTHER READING

On unauthorised improvements, see J. Wolffe, "Enrichment by improvements in Scots law", in Johnston and Zimmermann, ***Unjustified***

---

[1] See H.L. MacQueen and J.M Thomson, *Contract Law in Scotland*, 3rd edn (2012), paras 6.19–6.27.

Enrichment: Key Issues in Comparative Perspective (2002), Ch.15, and R. Evans-Jones, "Seeking 'imposed' enrichment in improvements—classification and general enrichment actions in mixed systems: Scotland and South Africa" (2008) 16 R.L.R. 18; while for unauthorised performance of another's obligations, see H.L. MacQueen, "Payment of another's debt", also in Johnston and Zimmermann, *Unjustified Enrichment: Key Issues in Comparative Perspective*, Ch.17, and L.J. Macgregor and N.R. Whitty, "Payment of another's debt, unjustified enrichment and *ad hoc* agency" (2011) 15 *Edinburgh L.R.* 57.

TAKINGS

Like the imposed enrichment cases discussed in the previous section, takings cases were commonly treated under the heading of recompense under pre-1990s enrichment law.[1] Another important dimension of the cases, is that all types of property—land, corporeal moveables, and money—appear to be covered. Intellectual property may be added to the list: infringers of intellectual property rights have been held liable to recompense the owners for gains made from their infringements, and today most of the statutory forms of intellectual property rights provide a remedy against infringers known as an "account of profits".[2]

A ground for holding enrichment by taking to be unjustified is therefore *the support and protection of property rights*, expressed as follows by the Scottish Law Commission (emphasis supplied):

> "The right of property or ownership carries with it the *exclusive* rights of use, consumption and disposal (*jus utendi, fruendi, abutendi*): the objective of the law in attributing the ownership of a thing to any individual is to allow him the *exclusive* exercise and enjoyment of these rights. Any enrichment which any other person acquires by exercising these rights without the owner's authority is therefore, in principle, unjustified. It follows that that person must restore to the owner the value which he would have had to pay if he had bargained for the benefits in question. *In such a case the defender's enrichment is unjustified because it contradicts the objectives pursued by the law of property.*"[3]

But the law in this area may go further than the protection of property rights and also recognise, in at least some cases, taking of, or interference with, rights in general as a form of enrichment. The law of fiduciary obligations provides an important example.[4] Fiduciaries such as trustees, agents,

---

[1] Although note that restitution could be used in some cases: see pp.57–58.
[2] *Mellor v William Beardmore & Co Ltd*, 1927 S.C. 597; *Levin v Caledonian Produce* (Holdings) Ltd, 1975 S.L.T. (Notes) 69; Copyright, Designs and Patents Act 1988 ss.96(2) (copyright), 229(2) (unregistered design rights); Patents Act 1977 s.61(1)(d); Trade Marks Act 1994 s.14(2).
[3] Scottish Law Com. DP No.95, para.3.115.
[4] On fiduciary obligations in general see Gloag and Henderson, *The Law of Scotland* (2012), para.3.03.

partners and company directors are liable to hand over to those to whom their duties are owed, any gain that they make as a result of abusing their fiduciary position. This is because fiduciaries are supposed to act only in the interests of these creditors (the trust beneficiaries, the principal, the other partners, or the company, as the case may be), and not in their own interest.

Teacher v Calder
(1899) 1 F. (H.L.) 39

> In this Scottish case T loaned £15,000 to C for investment in the latter's timber business, in return for interest and a half-share in the net profits of that business. In breach of contract, C used the money for other purposes, making a substantial profit as a result; but he was able to repay T with the interest and the half-share of the timber profits over the period of the advance. The House of Lords held that T was not entitled to claim the gain which C had made from the breach of contract; their relationship was not fiduciary.

But this decision must now be seen in light of another, more modern decision of the House of Lords in an English case:

Attorney-General v Blake
[2001] 1 A.C. 268

> B was a member of the British intelligence service who betrayed his country and fled to the then Soviet Union. His memoirs were subsequently published in the UK and made a substantial profit. The Government sought to prevent these profits being transferred to B, and succeeded in doing so on the basis that the publication was a breach of B's lifelong contractual obligation to keep secret his activities as a spy. This, however, was not a fiduciary obligation, although close to it.

It remains to be seen how far this decision affects *Teacher v Calder*, to which the speeches of the Law Lords in *Blake* make no reference, and whether it has created a general right to recover enrichment arising from breach of contract regardless of whether economically measurable loss has occurred.[1] Blackie and Farlam point out that the Court of Appeal in *Blake* distinguished *Teacher* on grounds of remoteness—the difference between a breach which merely gave an opportunity for gain (*Teacher*) and one where the gain followed "directly" from the breach—and that this limit on recovery was accepted by Lord Nicholls in the House of Lords, albeit without reference to *Teacher*; accordingly they consider that "whether convincing or not, this distinction removes any absolute bar to claims in Scots law."[2]

---

[1] See further below, pp.68–69.
[2] J. Blackie and I. Farlam, "Enrichment by act of the party enriched", in *Mixed Legal Systems in Comparative Perspective: Property and Obligations in Scotland and South Africa*, Zimmermann, Visser and Reid (eds) (2004), pp.493–494.

A different ground for considering enrichment by taking to be unjustified may therefore be that *by the act of taking the enriched person committed, or benefited from, a wrong* of some kind: not necessarily a crime or a delict, but an act which for the purposes of enrichment law is characterised as a wrong (e.g. breach of a fiduciary obligation or, possibly after the *Blake* case, of a contract). Wrongdoing, which is neither criminal nor delictual in nature, but is nonetheless identified as such by the law, may explain why the consequential enrichments are recoverable. Or, it may be that these instances of reversing enrichment are to be linked to a policy of ensuring high standards of probity amongst fiduciaries (where it is certainly necessary, given the basic principle that the obligation is to pursue the interests of others and not to promote one's own), and amongst certain types of contracting parties, such as members of the intelligence services, where there is a clear public interest in preventing abuse of position for personal gain, rather than to general concepts of unjustified enrichment as such. Further, given the apparently continuing authority of *Teacher v Calder*,[1] the decision in *Blake* may not be part of the general Scots law of either enrichment or contract; and fiduciary obligations may be a distinct chapter of the law in some ways similar to, but nevertheless separate from, both unjustified enrichment and contract. But until these propositions are made clear by decided cases, caution suggests that enrichment by taking should be seen as unjustified, not only when it arises from misuse of another's property, but also when it results from wrongdoing of a kind recognised by other branches of the law such as contract and fiduciary obligations. This is supported by the DCFR's recognition of liability for use of another's asset "especially where the enriched person infringes the disadvantaged person's rights or legally protected interests", which is clearly not limited to the protection of property rights.[2]

Either a property or a wrongs-based understanding of the justification for enrichment liability explains why a business has no claim against a competitor who, in the ordinary course of business, succeeds in attracting away the former's customers (above, p.1). The first business has no property right in its customers, and competition must be unfair—for example, by way of misrepresenting or passing off one's goods or services as those produced by another—before any wrong is done.[3] The following case provides another useful example of recovery under this head being denied:

---

[1] (1899) 1 F. (H.L.) 39; and see above, p.48.

[2] DCFR VII.-4:101(c).

[3] See e.g. the Israeli case of *AShIR Import, Production and Distribution v Forum Avisarim and Consumption Products Ltd* (1998) 52(4) PD 289. For passing off, see Gloag & Henderson, *The Law of Scotland*, 13th edn (2012), para.33.02. It is not clear whether an enrichment claim is available in relation to passing off, but in principle there seems to be no objection (*Stair Memorial Encyclopaedia* (1993), Vol.15, para.1400).

Crewpace v French
[2011] CSOH 133; 2012 S.L.T. 126

C was the owner of one plot of ground and Mr and Mrs F the owners
of an adjoining plot. The two plots were the subject of a single
agricultural lease held by RF Co, of which the Fs were the directors.
The Fs granted another long lease over part of their plot and sold two
other parts of the ground, without the knowledge or consent of C. C
sought recompense of the Fs' resultant enrichment on the basis of
wrongful interference with its interest as a joint landlord. The claim
failed. C had no relevant interest in the ground owned by the Fs,
whose enrichment was justified by their ownership of the lands in
question.

FURTHER READING

For enrichment by takings, see K.G.C. Reid, "Unjustified enrichment and
property law" 1994 *Juridical Review* 167; A.J.M. Steven, "Recompense
for interference in Scots law" 1996 *Juridical Review* 50; J.W.G. Blackie,
"Enrichment, wrongs and invasion of rights in Scots law" [1997] *Acta
Juridica* 284, and J. Blackie and I. Farlam, "Enrichment by act of the party
enriched", in ***Mixed Legal Systems in Comparative Perspective: Property
and Obligations in Scotland and South Africa***, R. Zimmermann, D. Visser
and K. Reid (eds) (2004).

UNJUSTIFIED ENRICHMENTS OUTSIDE TRANSFERS,
IMPOSITIONS AND TAKINGS?

There are some cases where the Scottish courts have allowed enrichment
recovery but the facts are difficult to fit into the structure of transfer,
imposition and taking outlined in the preceding paragraphs. Most, perhaps
all, of these are three-party or indirect enrichment cases. The most notable
examples in the cases already discussed in this book are *M&I Instrument
Engineers Ltd v Varsada*[1]; and *Mercedes-Benz Finance Ltd v Clydesdale
Bank Plc*.[2] For their facts, see above, pp.22–23. In neither case can the
enriched person be seen as a transferee, or as someone who has been
imposed upon. There may be some analogy with takings cases. In *Varsada*,
B could be seen as one who had used another's property; but the money
which V fraudulently obtained was probably his at the time he gave it to B,
so the analogy ultimately fails. In the *Mercedes* case, the bank was in
possession of funds legitimately transferred to it by a third person, and its
enrichment lay in *withholding* money due to be transferred on again under

---

[1] *M&I Instrument Engineers Ltd v Varsada*, 1991 S.L.T. 106.
[2] *Mercedes-Benz Finance Ltd v Clydesdale Bank Plc*, 1997 S.L.T. 905.

the direct debit arrangement with the impoverished person. It is however reasonably clear in both cases that the defenders had no legal ground for retaining the money against the enrichment claim of the pursuers (i.e. the enrichment was *sine causa*). This underlines the importance of the basic enrichment principle stated by the Scottish courts in the 1990s. The starting point is whether enrichment may be retained on legal grounds; and this leaves open the possibility of recognising new types of claim not necessarily readily fitting the established patterns of liability, and, indeed, of accepting that former exclusions from liability must now be overturned.

5. DEFENCES

There has been much less discussion of defences in enrichment actions than of the grounds on which enrichment will be found unjustified. In part, this is because some defences are implicit within the discussion of the grounds: whether or not there is enrichment, whether it is "at the expense of" the pursuer, whether or not it is "indirect", whether or not there is a legal ground such as gift or contract to justify the retention of the enrichment, whether or not a transferor knew that the transfer was undue, and so on. But the recognition that a general principle against unjustified enrichment underlies the whole subject, does imply a need to consider whether there are also distinct defences arising after the grounds of action are established, the substance of which can be defined in their own right; and how far these defences are general for all unjustified enrichments.

EQUITY

It has long been stated in Scots law that enrichment remedies are equitable in nature,[1] meaning, not that they supplement the ordinary law in the English sense, but rather that the court may take account of, and balance, all factors affecting the relationship between the parties before deciding to order the restoration of or payment for enrichment. In other words, the overall equities of the case may mean that the enrichment stays where it is, even though all the positive requirements for recovery are met.[2] Thus, for example, in the case of *Varney v Burgh of Lanark*[3] (above, p.15), it was inequitable to allow the builder to recover for the sewers it had installed instead of the local authority, because the parties had been in dispute about liability to perform this act and the builder had had available at the time a remedy—an action for implement of a statutory duty—by which the dispute

---

[1] See, e.g. *Bell v Thomson* (1867) 6 M. 64 at 69; *Lawrence Building Co v Lanarkshire County Council*, 1978 S.C. 30 at 41–42.
[2] See *Morgan Guaranty Trust Co of New York v Lothian Regional Council*, 1995 S.C. 151 at 165–166, per Lord President Hope.
[3] *Varney v Burgh of Lanark*, 1974 S.C. 245.

could have been resolved. Again, in cases about unauthorised payment of another's debt, equity might allow the debtor to plead against the recovery-seeking payer the defences that would have been available against the creditor or the creditor's assignee.[1] Some former defences, such as the inexcusability of the impoverished person's error, have now been subsumed within the wider concept of equity, becoming merely factors in the balancing process.[2] On the other hand, a number of more specific concepts have emerged from the cases and writings on the subject, although often these cannot yet be seen as highly refined and worked out specific defences. The main example is change of position, sometimes also known as loss of enrichment.

CHANGE OF POSITION/LOSS OF ENRICHMENT[3]

A party who has spent, consumed or otherwise disposed of an enrichment, and is, therefore, no longer enriched, may be able to escape liability to restore or pay for it, in whole or in part. The approach to be taken is outlined by Lord Kyllachy in *Credit Lyonnais v George Stevenson & Co Ltd*:

> "[T]he defenders, in order to establish such a defence, would require to show (1) that they had reasonable grounds for believing that the money was theirs; and (2) that having that reasonable belief, they acted upon it so as to alter their position in such manner as to make repetition unjust."[4]

Such a defence has been recognised in older *condictio indebiti* and CCDCNS cases. It also explains why in takings cases, where a recipient of moveable property has transferred it to a third party, the former's liability to the true owner is normally limited to his profit on the transaction, unless he has acted in bad faith or is at fault (see below, pp.57–58). Where the enrichment is by way of a saving, it can never be lost, so the defence does not apply in such cases.

See also the hard but salutary case of:

---

[1] See above, p.46.
[2] See above, p.28, and note the case of *Bank of New York v North British Steel Group*, 1992 S.L.T. 613.
[3] DCFR VII.-6:101 calls this defence "disenrichment" and makes it unavailable if the enriched person has obtained a substitute for the enrichment, or (subject to exceptions) was not in good faith at the time of the disenrichment. One of the exceptions is disenrichment by force majeure, so long as the enriched person was in good faith at the time of enrichment.
[4] *Credit Lyonnais v George Stevenson & Co Ltd* (1901) 9 S.L.T. 93 at 95.

Royal Bank of Scotland v Watt
1991 S.C. 48

For the facts, see above, p.8. In defence to RBS's claim for repayment, W argued that he no longer had the money, having given it to the rogue. The court rejected the defence, as W had been negligent, and therefore an order for repetition was not unjust.

SUBSIDIARITY

Under the pre-1990s law of recompense there was a defence of subsidiarity which meant that a claim of recompense would not succeed if some other claim or procedure was open to the pursuer in the situation.[1] The best-known example was the case of *Varney v Burgh of Lanark* (above, p.15) where as already noted an action of recompense was not allowed to a contractor who had performed a local authority's statutory obligation to connect a housing development to the sewage system, because there was available another action by which the authority could have been compelled to perform its duty.[2] But the modern restructuring of enrichment law brought the continuing role of subsidiarity into question. The concept was applied in *Renfrewshire Council v McGinlay* (above, p.24), although the refusal of recovery in that case is probably better analysed on the basis that the defender's enrichment was indirect.[3] The defence was also successful in the following case:

Transco Plc v Glasgow City Council
2005 S.L.T. 958

G had a statutory duty to maintain a bridge although it had been closed to traffic. T had a statutory obligation to provide and maintain gas pipelines, two of which were carried over a river by the bridge in question. In order to minimize the risk to public safety and their pipelines resulting from the bridge's deterioration T carried out remedial works costing nearly £1 million and claimed recompense from G. *Held*: that T had had the alternative of suing G for implement of its statutory duty, and that T's self-help approach had short-cut proper procedure. Although G was enriched by T's activities, a claim of recompense was not available where the pursuer had an alternative remedy.

---

[1] See in particular *Stair Memorial Encyclopaedia*, Vol. 15, paras 68–71.

[2] See also *Bennett v Carse*, 1990 S.L.T. 454; *NV Devos Gebroeder v Sutherland Sportswear Ltd*, 1990 S.C. 291. For an earlier example, see *Northern Lighthouse Commissioners v Edmonston* (1908) 16 S.L.T. 439.

[3] See also the criticism of the decision by R. Evans-Jones, *Unjustified Enrichment*, paras 7.44, 8.117.

The academic analysis of this decision suggests that subsidiarity is not a general defence across the whole of enrichment law but is rather one which applies principally (if not exclusively) to cases of imposed enrichment by performance of another's non-monetary obligation.[1] But the answer to many other questions remains unclear. Must the alternative to enrichment be one practically as opposed to theoretically available to the impoverished party? For example, in the *Transco* case the council could have avoided its statutory duty by the simple expedient of de-listing the bridge, so G's alternative remedy would have been easily frustrated. Again, how far must the impoverished party search for an alternative remedy before launching an enrichment claim? Is it only necessary to look for a remedy against the enriched party, or must possible remedies against third parties be taken into account as well? The preferable approach would be to give subsidiarity a narrow role that prevents parties from forcing enrichment upon others where there are alternative practical channels by which the desired result can be achieved. There is no equivalent to subsidiarity in the DCFR, although there are articles about the interaction between enrichment and other legal rules.[2]

BONA FIDE PERCEPTION AND CONSUMPTION

This is a defence of some importance in all cases where enrichment arises from possession of property, whether by transfer or taking. The bona fide and enriched possessor[3] is generally liable to restore, not only the thing possessed, but also its fruits and accessions during his possession; but the identification and exploitation of such fruits and accessions during that time will usually avoid this liability.

---

[1] N. R. Whitty, "*Transco Plc v Glasgow City Council*: developing enrichment law after *Shilliday*" (2006) 10 *Edinburgh L.R.* 112; followed in Gloag & Henderson *The Law of Scotland* (2012), para.24.19, and H.L. MacQueen, "Unjustified enrichment, subsidiarity and contract", in V.V. Palmer and E. Reid (eds), *Mixed Jurisdictions Compared: Private Law in Louisiana and Scotland* (2009), pp.339–341, 343–345. See also M. Hogg, *Obligations* (2006), paras 4.120–122. *Corrie v Craig*, 2013 G.W.D. 1-55, where the pursuer had an alternative remedy under the March Dykes Act 1661, may provide another example in the modern case law, although subsidiarity is not discussed in the case. See further the case note by M. Hogg, 2013 S.L.T. (News) 111.

[2] See DCFR VII.-7:101–7:102.

[3] This does not include the improver in bona fide possession of another's property, since he is impoverished and is the pursuer, not the enriched defender; but the improver's enrichment claim will be offset by the fruits and accessions he has perceived and consumed during his possession.

OTHER DEFENCES[1]

Examples of other defences include personal bar,[2] prescription,[3] and compensation in the sense of set-off of the enriched person's claims against the impoverished person's enrichment claim (e.g. damages in some contract cases,[4] counter-enrichment claims[5]). When parties compromise or settle a dispute between themselves in order to avoid litigation, each surrendering some aspect of the rights they claim, resultant transfers cannot be later unseated as undue.

FURTHER READING

See generally R. Evans-Jones, *Unjustified Enrichment, Enrichment by Deliberate Conferral: Condictio* (2003), Ch.10. On the defence of change of position, see G.C. Borland, "Change of position in Scots law" 1996 S.L.T. (News) 139; P. Hellwege, "The scope of application of change of position in the law of unjust enrichment: a comparative study" (1999) 7 R.L.R. 92; and G.C. Borland, "Fault in the change of position defence" 2006 *Juridical Review* 89.

---

6. REMEDIES AND MEASURES OF RECOVERY

In *Shilliday v Smith*,[6] Lord President Rodger emphasised the characterisation of the "three R's" of Scots enrichment law—repetition, restitution, and recompense—as remedies, and earlier in this book (above, p.16) it was shown how these fitted together with the various forms of enrichment. Repetition is the remedy for the return of money, restitution that for the return of corporeal property, and recompense that for other forms of enrichment. *Shilliday* shows how the remedies may be drawn together in a single case: recompense for the materials and work which the pursuer paid for, repetition for the money which she paid directly to the defender.

---

[1] See generally Scot. Law Com. DP No.95, Vol.2, pp.63–95.
[2] See E. Reid and J. Blackie, *Personal Bar* (2006), Ch.12.
[3] See Prescription and Limitation (Scotland) Act 1973 Sch.1, para.1(b)—obligation to redress unjustified enrichment prescribes five years after it became enforceable, that is, when an enrichment becomes unjustified. See D Johnston, *Prescription and Limitation*, 2nd edn (2012), paras 4.88–4.90. That may be later than the occurrence of the enrichment (e.g. in cases of *causa data causa non secuta*), a point not fully analysed in some recent decisions such as *Thomson v Mooney* [2012] CSOH 177 and *Virdee v Stewart* [2011] CSOH 50.
[4] See further below, p.69.
[5] See for the court ordering the payer-pursuer to restore benefits received from the defender-payee as a condition of obtaining repetition, e.g. *North British and Mercantile Insurance Co v Stewart* (1871) 9 M. 534; *Haggarty v Scottish TGWU*, 1955 S.C. 109 at 114, 115.
[6] *Shilliday v Smith*, 1998 S.C. 725; see above, p.4.

It is again useful to turn to the distinction between enrichments by transfer, imposition, and taking.

TRANSFER

In repetition cases, generally the amount of money received must be returned, with interest running from the date of the initial transfer, while in restitution of property the thing transferred must be returned with fruits and accessions (subject to the defence of bona fide perception and consumption—above, p.54).[1] In *Findlay v Monro*,[2] a person who consumed goods delivered to him in error was found liable to restore their value. Recompense may be payable where the transfer is by way of services rendered or expenditure on the defender's interests, and the amount will be the value of the increase of assets or of the loss avoided for the defender.

IMPOSITION

The remedy in property improvement cases is recompense, and the measure of recovery is the amount by which the defender is enriched, limited by the amount the improver has spent. The amount of the enrichment will be the enhanced permanent value of the property arising from the improvements carried out during the good faith possession, as determined at the date the good faith ceases or the true owner resumes possession.

In cases of payment of another's debt, the amount due is the amount of the debt discharged with interest from the date of the payment, while in performance of another's non-money obligation, the amount of the enrichment is due.

TAKING

The remedial situation is most complex in cases of enrichment by taking of another's property. Awards may be in relation to the value of the use, the value of the property taken, or the profit made from the use, depending on the circumstances of the case.

Use of another's property attracts liability to pay a reasonable sum, which may be measured by, for example, market rents, the annual worth of the land, or the expenditure saved by the user through having the use in question. The taker of funds may also be liable in repetition, repaying the amount taken.

---

[1] In *Mactaggart & Mickel Homes Ltd v Hunter* [2010] CSOH 130 the Lord Ordinary (Hodge) accepted (at paras 101–104) that restitution could extend to the re-conveyance to the pursuers of heritable property transferred by them for a purpose that failed.

[2] *Findlay v Monro*, 1698 Mor. 1707; see above, p.9.

Where the defender cannot return a thing because he has consumed, destroyed or sold it in good faith and acting with due care, generally the remedy is recompense and the defender is liable to the extent of his enrichment. The defender's enrichment liability continues to apply even if the pursuer can recover the thing itself from a third party to whom the defender had transferred it.[1]

> Example: A lets a car to B on hire purchase terms. Before completing the hire purchase payments B sells the car to a dealer C, who resells at a profit to another dealer D. A is able to recover the car itself from D and also C's profit from the resale to D. There is no "double recovery" here in A having claims against both C and D. C has been enriched by its use of another's property, while the property itself has also been recovered by the owner A.[2]

The case described below shows, however, that bad faith or fault will make the taker-defender liable for the full value of the thing. This remedy is usually taken to be a surrogate form of restitution.

Faulds v Townsend
(1861) 23 D. 437

> A manufacturing chemist bought for 12/- (60p), around midnight but in the course of its business, a horse, which was immediately killed and boiled up for use in manufacture, producing a profit of about 10/- (50p). The horse, it turned out, had previously been stolen and was worth £10. *Held*: that the chemist was liable to the true owner for the full value of the horse. Although not in bad faith, there had been fault and lack of due care in checking the antecedents of the horse.

Further, where the defender so used the pursuer's property as to cause himself or a third party to gain title to it by original acquisition (e.g. by specification), the pursuer will recover the value of the property he has lost, not the defender's enrichment or the value of the new property. The defender's good faith makes no difference to this outcome, which is an effect of property law.[3]

Oliver & Boyd v The Marr Typefounding Co Ltd
(1901) 9 S.L.T. 170

> OB employees stole type from their employers, and by various subsequent transactions the type ended up with MT, who were in good faith. MT melted down the type (this being held to amount to specification, the creation from earlier materials of a new subject,

---

[1] Gloag & Henderson *The Law of Scotland* (2012), para.24.20; *Harper Collins Publishers Ltd v Young* [2007] CSOH 65; A.J.M. Steven (2007) 11 *Edinburgh L.R.* 411.

[2] Based on *North-West Securities Ltd v Barrhead Coachworks Ltd*, 1976 S.C. 68 (above, p.13).

[3] On specification see Gloag & Henderson *The Law of Scotland* (2012), para.31.12; Gretton and Steven, *Property, Trusts and Succession* (2009), para.8.22.

which is owned by the specificator) and resold it. *Held*: that MT were liable to OB for the full value of the type.

International Banking Corporation v Ferguson, Shaw & Sons
1910 S.C. 182

FS bought refined cotton seed oil in good faith, and turned it into lard, which was then resold at a profit. But the party from whom the oil had been purchased had not had good title, and IBC, the true owners, sued FS as specificators for the full value of the oil. *Held*: FS were liable for the full value of the oil.

ENRICHMENT REMEDIES PERSONAL, NOT PROPRIETARY

In contrast with English law, the Scots law enrichment remedies have only personal and not proprietary effects. The importance of this is when the defender is insolvent and does not have enough money to pay all its creditors in full. The enrichment creditor has no right to be paid in full ahead of any other unsecured or preferential creditor. While the Scots law of trusts has a process of "tracing", better known as "real subrogation", this permits no more than identification of property held by the trustees and acquired with the proceeds from selling other trust property, and brings the property so identified under the trust. Unlike its English namesake, this "tracing" does not support any other proprietary claim to the sum thus identified or any assets acquired by use of the money. Likewise, the Scottish recognition of the "constructive trust" appears to be limited to the special case of a person acquiring trust property from trustees otherwise than as a trust beneficiary or for value, who is regarded as holding the property as trustee for the original trust. It is thus not as far reaching as the English constructive trust, which may apply to property not originally subject to any trust the acquisition of which makes the recipient unjustly enriched.[1]

Scots law instead applies its principle against a person profiting from another's fraud or breach of trust or fiduciary duty by allowing a personal claim in recompense against a person receiving an asset from the wrongdoer if that person is in bad faith (i.e. with knowledge of the fraud or breach of duty) or is a donee (i.e. gave no consideration for what was received). What the profited person acquired from the wrongdoer must be the same as what the latter earlier acquired wrongfully from the pursuer, or a substitute to which the pursuer has title by virtue of the rules on tracing.[2]

---

[1] See D.R. Macdonald, "Restitution and property law" 1988 S.L.T. (News) 81; G.L. Gretton, "Constructive trusts" (1997) 1 *Edinburgh L.R.* 281, 408 (two parts); P. Hood, "What is so special about being a fiduciary?" (2000) 4 *Edinburgh L.R.* 308. For recent cases touching on some of the issues see *J.S. Cruickshank (Farmers) Ltd v Gordon & Innes Ltd (in receivership)* [2007] CSOH 113; *Macadam v Grandison* [2008] CSOH 53; *Commonwealth Oil & Gas Co Ltd v Baxter* [2009] CSIH 75; 2010 S.C. 156.

[2] See N. R. Whitty, "The 'no profit from another's fraud' rule and the 'knowing receipt' muddle" (2013) 17 *Edinburgh L.R.* 37, criticising in particular *Commonwealth Oil & Gas Co Ltd v Baxter* [2009] CSIH 75; 2010 S.C. 156 (on which see also D.J. Carr, (2010) 14 *Edinburgh L.R.* 273 and R. Evans-Jones [2010] R.L.R. 173).

Two cases illustrate these points.[1]

Raymond Harrison & Co's Trustee v North-West Securities Ltd
1989 S.L.T. 718

Cattle were sold in breach of a hire purchase agreement, with the proceeds of the sale ending up in the hands of a firm subsequently sequestrated. It was held that the original owner of the cattle had no preferential claim to these proceeds in the sequestration, in part because there was still a claim to recover the cattle themselves from the third party purchaser.

M & I Instrument Engineers Ltd v Varsada and Beattie
1991 S.L.T. 106

A obtained £50,000 from B by fraud and applied the funds to the purchase of a house in the name of his mistress C. B being unable to recover from A claimed from C and was held entitled to repayment of the £50,000, on the basis that no-one was entitled to profit from the fraud of another. B's claim was however clearly a personal one only, for repayment of the money, not a proprietary one to the house bought with the fraudulently procured funds.

RESTITUTION AND VINDICATION

While it is clear that enrichment remedies are personal and not proprietary in Scots law, the remedy of restitution is equally clearly a means by which a party may ultimately be able to regain ownership of a thing. If something belonging to me comes into other, unauthorised hands, but I remain owner (e.g. after theft), my action for recovery of the property is one of vindication rather than restitution. Strictly speaking, I only need an enrichment action to recover the property if the transfer or taking has made the other person owner, since otherwise I have suffered no loss and the holder is not enriched. The effect of a successful enrichment claim will be to give the pursuer the personal right to be re-vested with ownership of the restored property. Stair long ago recognised, however, that an owner might make a claim of restitution, and the theoretically pure position just outlined is often ignored or overlooked in practice.[2] Similar issues arise where a person is in lawful possession of an object: unauthorised dispossession is remedied by the possessory action of spuilzie, while a transfer of possession to another in error, or for a purpose which fails, gives rise to a claim for restitution.

FURTHER READING

See Evans-Jones, *Unjustified Enrichment, Enrichment by Deliberate Conferral: Condictio* (2003), Ch.9.

---

[1] See also *Mercedes-Benz Finance Ltd v Clydesdale Bank Plc*, 1997 S.L.T. 905 (above, p.23).
[2] Stair, *Institutions*, I,7,2. See further K.G.C. Reid, "Unjustified enrichment and property", 1994 *Juridical Review* 167.

7. FLOWCHART OF UNJUSTIFIED ENRICHMENT IN TWO-PARTY CASES*

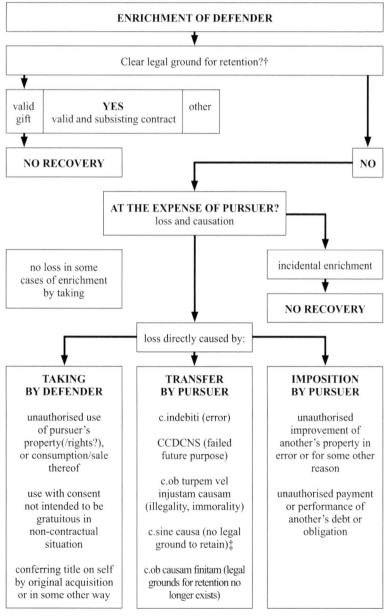

ENRICHMENT OF DEFENDER

Clear legal ground for retention?†

| valid gift | **YES** valid and subsisting contract | other |

NO RECOVERY

NO

AT THE EXPENSE OF PURSUER?
loss and causation

no loss in some cases of enrichment by taking

incidental enrichment

NO RECOVERY

loss directly caused by:

TAKING BY DEFENDER	**TRANSFER BY PURSUER**	**IMPOSITION BY PURSUER**
unauthorised use of pursuer's property(/rights?), or consumption/sale thereof	c.indebiti (error) CCDCNS (failed future purpose)	unauthorised improvement of another's property in error or for some other reason
use with consent not intended to be gratuitous in non-contractual situation	c.ob turpem vel injustam causam (illegality, immorality) c.sine causa (no legal ground to retain)‡	unauthorised payment or performance of another's debt or obligation
conferring title on self by original acquisition or in some other way	c.ob causam finitam (legal grounds for retention no longer exists)	

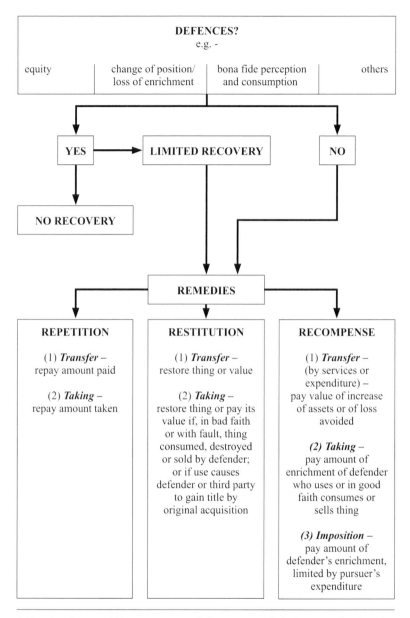

---

* This flowchart would become very tangled were it to include the topic of 'indirect' or multi-party enrichment, which is accordingly excluded.

† This aspect could equally well appear amongst the defences.

‡ Note this is the second appearance of 'without legal ground' in this flowchart, illustrating the still incomplete analysis of Scots law on this issue.

8. UNJUSTIFIED ENRICHMENT AND OTHER BRANCHES OF THE LAW

This book has indicated several times the key principle, that a person who is enriched can only retain it if the benefit is justified by some legal ground such as a gift or a contract. This section explores the principle further, by considering these legal grounds for retention of enrichment in more detail. Others might include the conferral of a benefit under a trust or a legacy, payments received as the result of a court order, and payment in response to a lawful demand for tax. Unjustified enrichment can only be understood in relation to these other branches of law.

GIFT (DONATION)[1]

Few cases illustrate the justification of an enrichment as an unconditional gift. But the negative version of the proposition, namely, that an enrichment was conferred without intention to donate and is, therefore, reversible, is frequently found in the Institutional Writers and judicial dicta.[2] This has been particularly important in cases about use of and improvements to another's property, and about performance of another's obligation. The presumption against donation in Scots law is also relevant here. Conditional gifts (e.g. wedding presents) are, it is conceived, returnable if the condition fails (see further above, p.32).

A controversial case, where a gift was found not to be returnable as an unjustified enrichment, is *Masters and Seamen of Dundee v Cockerill*.[3]

Fraternity of Masters and Seamen of Dundee v Cockerill
(1869) 8 M. 278

> The FMSD was a charitable organisation, the members of which subscribed an annual fee, in return for which they and their dependents were entitled to certain payments if the member died or fell into financial difficulties. C, a member, went on a voyage from Dundee and was not heard of for 16 years. During that time, when it was believed that C was dead, his wife received support from FMSD in accordance with the rules of the organisation, and also the sum of 13 shillings (65p) in addition. When C returned, it was held that the support given under the rules, having been made under an error of

---

[1] On the law of donation see *Stair Memorial Encyclopaedia*, Reissue, "Donation" (W.M. Gordon); H.L. MacQueen and M.A. Hogg, "Donation in Scots law", 2012 *Juridical Review* 1.
[2] Stair, *Institutions*, 1.8.2, 6; Bankton, *Institute*, 1.9.1, 41; Bell, *Principles*, para.538; *Lawrence Building Co v Lanarkshire County Council*, 1978 S.C. 30 at 41, per Lord President Emslie.
[3] *Masters and Seamen of Dundee v Cockerill* (1869) 8 M. 278.

fact (that C was dead—see further below), should be repaid; but not the 13 shillings, since although it had been paid under the same mistake, it was a gift which FMSD had no legal obligation to make.

This case is controversial, because arguably the FMSD's mistake about C's death was as much an invalidation of the gift as it was of the payment under the rules. Gifts may be contracts, and the factors which invalidate contracts may often also invalidate gifts. In the *Dundee* case, the judges said that the FMSD would not have been able to recover the 13 shillings if, e.g., C's wife had unexpectedly become rich after the donation. But that situation, it is suggested, would not have involved an error of the kind required to trigger an enrichment claim for restoration of the gift, but was rather one of a misprediction as to uncertain future events, quite different in kind from the question of whether or not C was alive at the time of the donation (see further above, p.27). The result would certainly have been different if the 13 shillings had been paid conditionally, made for example on the basis that, if C returned, or if his wife remarried, it would be repayable; this would mean that the money was returnable upon the fulfilment of the condition.

CONTRACT

An enrichment, whether a saving or a gain, is justified if it arises through the performance of a valid and subsisting contract: legal grounds exist for the retention of such enrichment.[1] Note that this is not a matter of enrichment being subsidiary to contract, simply one of its justification.[2] The law of unjustified enrichment does not enable inquiries into whether too much or too little was paid for goods or services or any other performance supplied under a contract.

Dollar Land (Cumbernauld) Ltd v CIN Properties Ltd
1998 S.C. (H.L.) 90

Complex arrangements for the development of a shopping centre involved the establishment of a 125-year lease, between DLC as landlords and CIN as tenants for a nominal rent of £1 per year if asked, and a 99 year sub-lease back from CIN to DLC. The rent

---

[1] See in addition to the *Dollar Land* case described below *Castle Inns (Stirling) Ltd v Clark Contracts Ltd* [2006] S.C.L.R. 663; *Hanover (Scotland) Housing Association Ltd v Reid*, 2006 S.L.T. 518; *Duncan v American Express*, 2009 S.L.T. 112; and *Mactaggart & Mickel Homes Ltd v Hunter* [2010] CSOH 130.

[2] Compare DCFR VII.-2:101(1)(a): "An enrichment is unjustified unless … the enriched person is entitled as against the disadvantaged person to the enrichment by virtue of a contract … ."

payable by DLC was a 77.5 per cent proportion of the rents payable to them by the "occupational" sub-tenants of the shopping centre. DLC and their predecessors in title had made a contribution to the capital costs of developing the centre. CIN terminated the sub-lease for non-payment of rent by DLC. The sub-lease provided that on such termination CIN was entitled to enter on the premises and use, possess and enjoy the same free of all claims by DLC as tenants, as if the sub-lease had never been granted. This meant that CIN became entitled to 100 per cent of the occupational sub-tenant rents, while under the head lease DLC was only entitled to £1 per year. DLC claimed that CIN was in the circumstances unjustifiably enriched, the losses to DLC being wholly disproportionate to their breach of contract, and involving deprivation of any return on their capital investment. *Held*: that DLC had no enrichment claim. Lord Hope of Craighead said (at 94): "An obligation in unjustified enrichment is owed where the enrichment cannot be justified on some legal basis arising from the circumstances in which the defender was enriched. There can be no better justification for an enrichment than that it was obtained and is being retained in the exercise of a contractual right against the party who seeks to invoke the remedy ... . The benefit which has enriched CIN is one which was provided for them expressly in the contract of sublease."

But despite this general principle, there are a number of cases closely connected to the performance of contracts where enrichment law does become relevant.

The most obvious example is with regard to performances where a contract is null (or void); that is to say, although there appears to be a contract, it never had any existence in law as a result of some flaw in its formation, such as the lack of capacity, or an error, of one or more of the parties, or the use by one party against the other of overwhelming force or duress, or its illegality.[1] If, despite the nullity, performance is rendered, then it may be reversed or paid for under the law of enrichment, typically as an undue performance (see further, pp.26–31 above on the *condictio indebiti*).

Wilson v Marquis of Breadalbane
(1859) 21 D. 957
(contract void for dissensus on price)

Bullocks were delivered by A to B, but the parties could not agree on the price to be paid. It was held that there was no contract but that B, being unable to restore the cattle, had to pay their market value.

---

[1] See DCFR VII.-2:101(2): "If the contract ... is void, ... the enriched person is not entitled to the enrichment on that basis."

Came v City of Glasgow Friendly Society
1933 S.C. 69
(contract void for illegality)

C took out an assurance policy on the life of T (her step-mother). The contract contravened the Life Assurance Act 1774 and was accordingly void. C paid premiums for five years before the true position emerged. She then sought repayment of the premiums. The life assurance company was ordered to repay the premiums. The Second Division appears to have applied the principle *causa data causa non secuta*, on the basis that C did not get what she paid for. But it seems more correct to say that she did get what she wanted (a policy over T's life), and paid because she thought, wrongly, that she was due to do so; she should, therefore, be repaid under the *condictio indebiti* (see the opinion of Lord Hunter).

Morgan Guaranty v Lothian Regional Council
1995 S.C. 151
(contract void for lack of capacity)

For the facts, see above, p.9. Payments made in error under the void contract fell to be restored. Lord President Hope said (at 156): "[T]he payments were made in implement of a supposed obligation under a contract which was discovered not to exist, and the recipients of the payment were enriched because the payment was of money to which they were not entitled. Leaving aside any equitable considerations which might suggest that the defenders should keep the money, I would regard this as a clear case for a remedy on the ground of unjustified enrichment."

The position is, however, different where the contract is merely annullable (or voidable). Here the contract does take and retain legal effect until such time as it is annulled, or reduced, by court process. Therefore, performances rendered under it before its reduction are valid contractual performances and cannot be seen as undue for the purposes of the *condictio indebiti* (see above, pp.26–27). One of the conditions on which annulment will be allowed is that *restitutio in integrum* (restoration of the parties to their pre-contractual position) may be effected. Although this requirement of restoration looks like reversing or paying for enrichments, it is not viewed as a remedy for enrichment, but is rather a condition of annulment or reduction, and in working out what must be done, enrichment principles are not applied. This has been criticised[1]; were enrichment principles to be applied, the *condictio ob causam finitam* would provide the appropriate method of approach in Scots law.[2]

---

[1] R. Evans-Jones, *Unjustified Enrichment* (2003), para.9.125–134, argues that *restitutio in integrum* can be understood as based on unjustified enrichment.

[2] Cf. DCFR VII.-2:101(2): "If the contract … is … avoided or otherwise rendered ineffective retrospectively, the enriched person is not entitled to the enrichment on that basis."

Contractual obligations may be conditional, that is, they may become enforceable only upon the occurrence of external events not certain to happen (suspensive conditions); or alternatively they may cease to be enforceable upon the occurrence of such events.[1] Where the contract is subject to a suspensive condition that does not materialise, and as a result the defender comes under no obligation to supply the consideration, any pre-payment by the pursuer can be recovered. It is unclear whether this is on the basis of the CCDCNS, because the pursuer's payment was made for a future purpose,[2] or the *condictio indebiti*, because the contract being unenforceable the payment was not due.[3] A Louisiana case illustrates the situation.

Simon v Arnold
727 So 2d 699 (La, 1999)

Parties entered a contract under which they agreed to an immediate exchange of occupancy of their respective homes pending an exchange of titles to be completed in 12 months' time. One of the parties also agreed to take over the other's mortgage payments immediately, with that mortgage to be formally assumed at the same time as the titles were eventually exchanged. The arrangement thus made in fact continued for seven years without the title position ever being regularised, and the relationship then broke down. The court held that the initial agreement was subject to a suspensive condition which had failed to materialise, and the contract therefore failed. The party whose mortgage payments had been taken over was enriched at the other party's expense because the amount of her mortgage indebtedness had been reduced by some $7,000. The impoverished party was held entitled to recover this (rather than the $33,000 apparently paid to the lender) along with what he had spent on improvements to the property he had occupied under the initial agreement, found to amount to some $4,000.

Where a transfer is made under a contract subject to a resolutive condition which then materialises to dissolve the contract, the transfer falls to be restored under the *condictio ob causam finitam*, the purpose of the transfer having existed when it was made and ceased to do so afterwards.[4]

---

[1] See MacQueen & Thomson, *Contract Law in Scotland* (2012), paras 3.57–3.70 for discussion and examples.

[2] Gloag & Henderson *The Law of Scotland* (2012), para.24.13 (4), citing Voet 12.6.3 and *Brown v Nielson* (1825) 4 S. 271.

[3] In South Africa it has been held that the *condictio indebiti* applies rather than the CCDCNS: see Visser, *Unjustified Enrichment* (2008), p.287 and note, 536–538; Du Plessis, *South African Law of Unjustified Enrichment* (2012), pp.124–126, 181–182. See also R. Evans-Jones, *Unjustified Enrichment* (2003), paras 3.130–131 and 4.14 (but note failure of a suspensive condition does not necessarily make the whole contract void).

[4] Evans-Jones, *Unjustified Enrichment* (2003), paras 4.14, 4.18, 6.07.

As discussed earlier (above, pp.35–37), where a contract is discharged by frustration, and is, therefore, no longer subsisting, Scots law allows enrichment principles and remedies to govern what is to happen with regard to performances rendered under the contract which have not been met by the anticipated counter-performance as a result of the frustrating event. This is seen as a major instance of the CCDCNS, the classic case being *Cantiere San Rocco v Clyde Shipbuilding Co Ltd*.[1] As noted in the discussion of the case above (p.36), were the matter still open, the situation might be better treated as another instance of the *condictio ob causam finitam*. But in any event, whether unjustified enrichment provides the best way of dealing with cases of frustration is much debated, since it can seem one-sided in its approach and therefore unable to deal as finely as may be necessary with the fair adjustment of the parties' losses as well as their gains.[2]

Similar issues can arise in cases where the contract is terminated prematurely, because the material breach of one of the parties enables the other to exercise the contractual remedy of rescission. In many such cases, one result of rescission is mutual restitution: in sale of goods, for example, where the seller does not give good title to the goods, or where the seller supplies goods which are defective, the buyer is entitled to get the price back, while the goods fall to be returned to the seller (or to the true owner, where appropriate). It is not clear whether this restitution, after material breach, should be treated as governed by enrichment principles such as CCDCNS (or the *condictio ob causam finitam*), or is rather something like *restitutio in integrum*, a contractual remedy with some similarity to enrichment ones.[3] The latter seems the better view at present.[4] It seems that restitution cannot be claimed from the contract-breaker's assignee because, while an assignee is subject to the defences available against the cedent, counterclaims available against the cedent cannot be made against the assignee.[5]

---

[1] 1923 S.C. (H.L.) 105; see above, p.36.

[2] MacQueen & Thomson, *Contract Law in Scotland* (2012), para.4.85. See also *Lloyds TSB Foundation for Scotland v Lloyds Banking Group* [2013] UKSC 3, para.43, per Lord Hope of Craighead.

[3] As in South Africa: *Baker v Probert*, 1985 (3) S.A. 429 (A.).

[4] But see *Mactaggart & Mickel Homes Ltd v Hunter* [2010] CSOH 130, a case of termination by the buyer of a contract for the sale of land, where termination was justified under the contract itself but where the seller refused in breach of the contract to return a deposit and the buyer consequently did not re-convey the land. The buyer had a claim of damages against the seller for its breach, but the Lord Ordinary (Hodge) expressed the view obiter (paras 100–101) that had the value of the land exceeded the amount of the damages the seller would have had an enrichment claim. This claim would not have been precluded by the existence of a contract between the parties because that contract contained no provision on the matter (unlike the lease in the *Dollar Land* case, above, pp.63–64).

[5] *Compagnie Commerciale Andre SA v Artibell Shipping Co Ltd*, 2001 S.C. 653, following the English House of Lords decision, *Pan Ocean Shipping Ltd v Creditcorp Ltd (The Trident Beauty)* (1994) 1 W.L.R. 161; see also the sheriff court cases, *Binstock Miller & Co v Coia & Co*, 1957 S.L.T. (Sh.Ct) 47, and *Alex Lawrie (Factors) Ltd v Mitchell Engineering Ltd*, 2001 S.L.T. (Sh.Ct) 93. Compare the South African case, *LTA Engineering Co Ltd v Seacat Investments (Pty) Ltd* 1974 (1) S.A. 747 (A.), under which the assignee must "defend" the cedent if the assignation was made in bad faith to defeat the debtor's counter-claim (see also *Digest* 3.3.34).

Finally, at present a contract-breaker is not generally liable to account to the other contracting party for gains made as a result of the breach of contract;[1] but the English decision of *Attorney General v Blake*[2] has thrown this doctrine into doubt. The English courts have not treated *Blake* expansively, the few successful claims generally involving deliberate breaches of contract intended to make a gain or avoid a loss.[3] A gain-based remedy for breach of contract might provide a just solution in cases like *Ruxley Engineering v Forsyth*,[4] where a builder saved money by constructing a swimming pool that did not conform to the contractual specifications, but was liable for only nominal damages because the client had suffered no significant loss as a result of the breach. Another important example is *Wrotham Park Estate Co Ltd v Parkside Homes Ltd*,[5] where a developer built more than the contractually permitted number of houses on a piece of land: damages for breach were based on what the developer would have had to pay to get the restriction relaxed, with the major factor in the calculation being the developer's profit and the sum awarded being five per cent thereof.[6] MacQueen & Thomson comment as follows in their text on contract law:

> "From a Scottish point of view the attraction of the new remedy is its support for performance of the contract according to its terms: the taking away of gains made from breach gives parties an incentive to adhere to their contracts. On the other hand, if the remedy is limited to exceptional cases, it will in effect become a matter of judicial discretion rather than genuinely rule-based law, with all the consequential uncertainty for contracting parties; and if it is essentially a remedy against cynical or intentional breach aimed at making the gain in question, there will have to be difficult inquiries into the motivations lying behind people's conduct."[7]

---

[1] *Teacher v Calder* (1899) 1 F. (H.L.) 39.

[2] [2001] 1 A.C. 268; see above, p.48.

[3] *Esso Petroleum Co Ltd v Niad* [2001] All E.R. (D.) 324 (Nov.); *Experience Hendrix LLC v PPX Enterprises Inc.* [2003] EMLR 25 (C.A.). Unsuccessful claims include *AB Corporation v CD Company, The Sine Nomine* [2002] 1 Lloyd's Rep. 805; *World Wide Fund for Nature (formerly World Wildlife Fund) v World Wrestling Federation Entertainment Inc* [2002] F.S.R. 32, aff'd [2002] F.S.R. 33 (C.A.).

[4] [1996] A.C. 344.

[5] [1974] 1 W.L.R. 798.

[6] In *WWF World Wide Fund for Nature (formerly World Wildlife Fund) v World Wrestling Federation Inc. (No.2)* [2008] 1 W.L.R. 445 (C.A.) the controversial suggestion is made that the recovery in *Wrotham Park* was "compensatory" rather than gain-based. The approach is however apparently confirmed in the Privy Council decision, *Pell Frischmann Engineering Ltd v Bow Valley Iran Ltd* [2011] 1 W.L.R. 2370, where the defendants' gain from its breach of a confidentiality agreement was between $1 and $1.8 million, but the damages awarded were $2.5 million and explicitly stated to be compensatory in nature. This was reaffirmed in *Force India Formula One Team Ltd v 1 Malaysia Racing Team SDN BHD* [2012] EWHC 616 (Ch), [2012] R.P.C. 29, paras 375–387.

[7] MacQueen and Thomson, *Contract Law in Scotland* (2012), para.6.17. See further M. Hogg, *Obligations* (2006), paras 4.123–131.

It may finally be noted that claims of this kind have been allowed in Israel, but not in South Africa or, so far, in Louisiana.[1]

On the other side of the breach of contract coin, a group of cases shows that in some situations a party who has broken a contract and is, as a result of the doctrine of mutuality of contract, unable to raise an action under the contract for payment in respect of contractual performances rendered, may be able to make an enrichment claim instead; typically, again, by way of the principle of the CCDCNS.[2] It seems that a pre-condition of use of the enrichment remedy is that the contract has been terminated as a result of the breach; the claim is also subject, of course, to the other party's counterclaim of damages for breach of contract.[3] The classic case is, again, that of the builder who fails to complete, or completes defectively, but this time viewed from a different angle:[4]

Steel v Young
1907 S.C. 360

A builder deviated from its contract to build a house by using milled lime rather than the contractually specified cement mortar. The client refused to pay the whole contract price, although the difference in value between a house with cement mortar and one with milled lime was only £5, but the cost of repairing the defect, which would have entailed pulling the house down and rebuilding it, exceeded the original contract price. The client was occupying the house. The court held that the builder, being in material breach, had no claim for the contract price, but could use an alternative approach, based upon the client's enrichment at his expense.

---

[1] For Israel see the Supreme Court decision *Adras Building Material Ltd v Harlow and Jones GmbH* (1988) 42(1) PD 221 (fully translated in (1995) 3 R.L.R. 235) (seller of goods who re-sold to third party before delivery to first buyer liable to latter for gain from re-sale). For Louisiana see H. L. MacQueen, "Unjustified enrichment, subsidiarity and contract", in Palmer and Reid, *Mixed Jurisdictions Compared: Private Law in Louisiana and Scotland* (2009), p.336. For South Africa see Visser, *Unjustified Enrichment* (2008), pp.692–695, and Du Plessis, *South African Law of Unjustified Enrichment* (2012), pp. 368–371.

[2] See H.L. MacQueen, "Unjustified enrichment and breach of contract", 1994 *Juridical Review* 137 at 149–66.

[3] Where the breach is non-material, the contract-breaker will usually be able to sue for the price of the work done with a deduction for the cost of repairing the breach. See also *Wiltshier Construction (Scotland) Ltd v Drumchapel Housing Co-operative Ltd*, 2003 S.L.T. 443; and *Robertson Construction Central v Glasgow Metro LLP* [2009] CSOH 71.

[4] See in addition to the cases described below, *Ramsay v Brand* (1898) 25 R. 1212; *Forrest v Scottish County Investment Co Ltd*, 1915 S.C. 115, affirmed 1916 S.C. (H.L.) 28; and note the South African cases of *Hauman v Nortje*, 1914 A.D. 293 and *BK Tooling (Edms) Bpk v Scope Precision Engineering (Edms) Bpk* 1979 (1) S.A. 391 (A.).

Thomson v Archibald
1990 G.W.D. 26–1438 (Edinburgh Sheriff Court)

A builder abandoned its contract with the work only 45 per cent done, and the employer, having terminated the contract, had the work completed by a second contractor. The builder sued the employer successfully on the grounds that the latter was enriched by having 45 per cent of the work done without being contractually bound to pay for it.

The doctrine is not applicable only in building cases, however:[1]

Graham v United Turkey Red Co
1922 S.C. 533

G was an agent acting for UTR and paid by commission upon sales he made for the company. In July 1916 G went into breach of the UTR contract by starting to sell also the goods of a rival company. Upon discovery of this, UTR dismissed G, who sued for unpaid commission. It was held that, while he could not recover the contractual commission for sales made after July 1916, G had an enrichment claim in respect of such sales.

PEC Barr Printers Ltd v Forth Print Ltd
1980 S.L.T. (Sh.Ct) 118

B and F had a contract for typesetting. B delivered half the work, but F terminated the contract because B would be unable to complete the remainder in time. B claimed successfully for the value of the work delivered.

Zemhunt Holdings Ltd v Control Securities Plc
1992 S.C. 58

Land was sold at an auction, with a condition being payment by the purchasers of a deposit of 10 per cent of the purchase price. The purchasers duly paid the deposit, but failed to come up with the balance of the price on the due date. The vendors terminated the contract on the ground of the purchasers' material breach. The purchasers then claimed repayment of the deposit under the CCDCNS. In the Outer House, Lord Marnoch held that the deposit was an advance part-payment, and was not, therefore, forfeited as a

---

[1] See in addition to the cases described below *NV Devos Gebroeder v Sunderland Sportswear Ltd*, 1990 S.C. 291; *Dollar Land (Cumbernauld) Ltd v CIN Properties Ltd*, 1998 S.C. (H.L.) 90.

result of the breach; but, further, that the CCDCNS could not be invoked by a party in breach and so responsible for the failure of overall performance. In the Second Division, Lord Marnoch was reversed on the deposit point, which made it unnecessary to determine whether or not a purchaser in breach was entitled to restoration of his advance payment. In an important obiter dictum, however, Lord Morison indicated that he saw such a claim as legitimate, given the ability of the payee to counterclaim for damages for breach of contract.

Two other situations closely connected to contracts should be mentioned. One is where parties are negotiating but have not yet formed a contract. In practice negotiating parties often commence performance of the transaction without having reached the contractual stage, anticipating a successful outcome of their dealing. If, however, the contract is never concluded, then return of and payment for the performances rendered during the abortive negotiations will generally be a matter for enrichment law. This might be on the basis of either the *condictio indebiti* or the CCDCNS, or through use of another's property not intended to be gratuitous.[1] A second situation is what may be called over-performance of a contract—paying more than the contract price, or paying twice; supplying more than the required number of goods, or supplying what is meant to be the same consignment more than once; doing more work than is required under a contract. Enrichment law can be used to provide a fair answer to these types of situation, since the over-performance was not due: for example, by enabling the return of the over-payment or the extra goods.[2] But there can be difficulties in more complex situations:

Smiths Gore v Reilly
2003 S.L.T. (Sh.Ct.) 15

SG, chartered surveyors, advised their client A to pay invoices for professional services rendered to A by R, a consulting engineer, under a contract. The invoices were then found to be an overcharge. A recovered the amount of the overcharge from SG, and assigned to SG its claim against R. *Held*: that since A was no longer impoverished, its assignation could give SG no better right against R than A had (*assignatus utitur iure auctoris*); action against R dismissed. A criticism of this case might be that only *initial* loss corresponding to the defender's enrichment is needed, and so long as the defender

---

[1] See, e.g. *Microwave Systems (Scotland) Ltd v Electro-Physiological Instruments Ltd*, 1971 S.C. 140; *Site Preparations Ltd v Secretary of State for Scotland*, 1975 S.L.T. (Notes) 41 (both claims unsuccessful); *Shetland Islands Council v BP Petroleum Development Ltd*, 1990 S.L.T. 82 (relevant claim; see above, p.17, for possibility that this was an implied contract case); and *Chartered Brands Ltd v Elmwood Design Ltd*, Unreported, Edinburgh Sheriff Court, May 15, 2009, noted by M. Hogg (2009) 13 *Edinburgh L.R.* 130.

[2] See (1882) 19 S.L.R. 835.

retains the enrichment the liability survives, there being no equity in its favour (see above, pp.19, 51). There is no defence of loss of impoverishment comparable to that of mitigation in contract or delict. If A had sued both SG and R, the contractual or delictual claim against the former would be reduced by the amount obtained from the latter by way of the *condictio indebiti*; but in the absence of a claim against R, A had something to assign to SG. Note also that the case is not one of payment of another's debt, since SG paid to discharge its own obligation to A, not R's liability to A.

Sometimes, especially where the recipient has used or taken the benefit of the over-supply, there could be an enrichment by taking or use of another's property; but that situation may be better analysed as one of implied contract.[1]

The two situations, of performance during contract negotiations and over-performance of a contract, can coalesce in the case where parties reach the end of a long-term contract, such as a lease, while negotiating its renewal, and, pending that renewal, allow the relationship to continue. In the event that the negotiations are unsuccessful, so that no new contract is ever formed, then performances rendered during the post-contract period may be restored, or paid for, under enrichment law.[2] The situation may be either one of undue performance or unauthorised use of another's property.

FURTHER READING

On enrichment and contract in general, see two articles by H.L. MacQueen: "Unjustified enrichment, subsidiarity and contract", in *Mixed Jurisdictions Compared: Private Law in Louisiana and Scotland*, E. Reid and V.V. Palmer (eds) (2009); and "Contract, unjustified enrichment and concurrent liability: a Scots perspective" [1997] *Acta Juridica* 176. See also M. Hogg, *Obligations*, 2nd edn (2006), Ch.4. On void contracts note further A. **Rodger, "Recovering payments under void contracts in Scots law", in** *The Search for Principle: Essays in Honour of Lord Goff of Chieveley*, W.J. Swadling and G. Jones (eds) (2000); while on breach of contract, see H.L. MacQueen, "Unjustified enrichment and breach of contract", 1994 *Juridical Review* 139; J.A. Dieckmann and R. Evans-Jones, "The dark side of *Connelly v Simpson*", 1995 *Juridical Review* 90; and S. Miller, "Unjustified enrichment and failed contracts" in *Mixed Legal Systems in Comparative Perspective: Property and Obligations in Scotland and South Africa*, R. Zimmermann, D. Visser and K. Reid (eds) (2004). D. Visser, *Unjustified Enrichment* (2008), pp.90–113 responds critically to Miller's arguments, and J. du Plessis, *South African Law of Unjustified Enrichment* (2012), pp. 89–92, responds to Visser's.

---

[1] See above, p.17. Note also Sale of Goods Act 1979 s.30 (if recipient does not reject the over-supply of goods, the seller may charge him at the contract rate).

[2] See *Rochester Poster Services Ltd v AG Barr Plc*, 1994 S.L.T. (Sh.Ct) 2 (above, p.12).

9. BENEVOLENT INTERVENTION IN ANOTHER'S AFFAIRS *(NEGOTIORUM GESTIO)*

As is apparent from its Latin name *(negotiorum gestio)* meaning "management (or administration) of affairs", this part of the law of obligations also originated in Roman law.[1] By comparison with enrichment or contract, however, benevolent intervention is of rather narrow scope, and there is little case law to elaborate the statements of principle found in the Institutional Writers and subsequent literature.[2] There may accordingly be assistance to be obtained from the DCFR, Book V of which deals with the matter under the title "Benevolent Intervention in Another's Affairs".

The situation envisaged is one where the intervener (the *gestor*) steps in, without authority, to manage the affairs *(negotia)* of another (the principal or *dominus*) who is unable (through absence, ignorance, or incapacity such as mental disability[3]) to deal with them himself or to authorise others to do so.[4] This can range from the preservation of property, such as putting a lost or abandoned car in a garage,[5] or putting goods in danger in a war-zone into a place of safety,[6] or repairing or improving a house,[7] to the payment of the debts of the principal[8]; but Scots law has yet to apply the concept to the preservation of the life, health or well-being of the principal. There would seem no reason in principle why it could not do so, and such claims are admitted in other jurisdictions.[9]

Paterson v Greig
(1862) 24 D. 1370

A mother improved the heritable property of her eldest son, a pupil child with no father or tutor. She was held to be a benevolent intervener for the boy.

---

[1] See *Digest* 3.5; *Code* 2.18(19).
[2] Stair, *Institutions*, 1.8.3–5; Bankton, *Institute*, 1.9.22–27; Erskine, *Institutes*, 3.3.52–53; Hume, *Lectures*, Vol.3, pp.175–7; Bell, *Principles*, paras 540–541.
[3] Important legislation in this area—the Adults with Incapacity (Scotland) Act 2000—can be usefully supplemented by benevolent intervention rules. For a summary of the 2000 Act, see Gloag & Henderson *The Law of Scotland* (2012), para.43.07-43.15.
[4] DCFR Book V labels the *gestor* the "intervener" and the *dominus* the "principal".
[5] *SMT Sales and Services Co Ltd v Motor and General Finance Co Ltd*, 1954 S.L.T. (Sh.Ct) 107.
[6] *Kolbin v Kinnear*, 1931 S.C. (H.L.) 128.
[7] *Paterson v Greig* (1862) 24 D. 1370; *Fernie v Robertson* (1871) 9 M. 437.
[8] *Reid v Lord Ruthven* (1918) 55 S.L.R. 616.
[9] *Stair Memorial Encyclopaedia*, Vol.15, para.102.

Fernie v Robertson
(1871) 9 M. 437

A daughter improved the heritable property of her senile mother. She was held to be a benevolent intervener for the old lady.

SMT Sales and Services Co Ltd v Motor
and General Finance Co Ltd
1954 S.L.T. (Sh. Ct) 107

MGF let a car to W on hire purchase. The police found the car abandoned. W, who was behind on his instalment payments, said the car was stolen but did no more. The police, as required by statute, ordered SMT to remove the vehicle to its garage. SMT could not get W to collect and pay for the service and sued MGF as owners. *Held*: SMT was a benevolent intervener entitled to claim expenses from the owner of the car.

If the beneficiary is aware of the situation with which the intervener is trying to deal, and has never the less chosen not to act, the intervener has no claim under the principles of benevolent intervention and must make any claim under the law of enrichment. See for example:

Garriock v Walker
(1873) 1 R. 100

The master of a ship saved a putrefying cargo of whale blubber and whale heads by having it unloaded from the ship, cleaned and put into casks, creating a profit for the owner who had refused to accept responsibility in the situation. The master's claim lay in enrichment (the owner's saving) rather than benevolent intervention.

North British Railway Company v Tod
(1893) 9 Sh. Ct Rep. 326

T's horse was injured in transit and the pursuer railway company incurred veterinary and livery charges in dealing with the animal, the owner having refused to accept responsibility for it. The railway company's claim lay in enrichment (the owner's saving) rather than in benevolent intervention.

A difficult situation may be where the principal is ignorant of the situation but could reasonably be made aware of it before any action is taken by the intervener. The DCFR provides that an intervener must have a reasonable ground for acting and does not do so if there is a reasonable opportunity to discover the wishes of the principal.[1]

---

[1]   DCFR VII.-1:101. An example of the situation envisaged may be *Bank of Scotland v MacLeod Paxton Woolard & Co*, 1998 S.L.T. 258 (below, p.75).

As a result of the absence or inability of the principal, the actions of the intervener cannot be based upon a contract between the parties, nor has the intervention been otherwise authorised by the principal. Despite this lack of consent or authority, the principal is liable for the expenses and outlays incurred by the intervener in the course of the management. Note, then, that this is essentially a claim for loss rather than for any enrichment which the principal might have as a result of the other's intervention in his affairs.

To have a claim, however, the intervener must intend the intervention to be of benefit to the principal and, probably, to claim his expenses in achieving this. If the intervener also intended some benefit to himself, he may still recover his expenses; but if he was acting entirely in his own interests, the claim of benevolent intervention is generally excluded. If the intervener intended to donate his services to the principal, again there is no benevolent intervention. Given that there is a presumption against donation in Scots law, it would probably be for the principal to prove that a gift was intended, and otherwise it would be assumed that the intervener had not intended to act gratuitously.

Kolbin v Kinnear
1931 S.C. (H.L.) 128

K2 transported K1's goods from Archangel to England in 1919, rescuing them from the Red Army then closing in on the city. K2 was interested in the safety and eventual resale of the goods because they had had possession as K1's export agents and had already incurred charges in respect of them. *Held*: K2's mixed motives did not prevent them from claiming in benevolent intervention.

Bank of Scotland v MacLeod Paxton Woolard & Co
1998 S.L.T. 258

BoS discovered that funds put into an account and then drawn upon had been placed there and then paid on as part of a fraudulent money-laundering operation. After discovering the fraud, BoS incurred expense in defending an action brought by a party claiming under a draft made upon the fraudulent fund. In defending a further action against it by the victims of the fraud for repayment of the funds in question, BoS argued that it had acted as intervener for the victims in defending the earlier action and was entitled to deduct from any repayment to them its expenses in that earlier action. *Held*: that the victims had been available at the time the first action was brought, and BoS could have sought their instructions on how to deal with the claim. Accordingly they had acted entirely in their own interests in incurring the expenditure, which could not be claimed under the head of benevolent intervention.

The intervener's action must be of at least initial utility to the principal.

This does not mean that the situation must be one of emergency or necessity,[1] but rather that the intervener's action is useful to the principal at the time of the intervention.

The classic illustration of benevolent intervention is where you find my house burning down while I am away on holiday. Your attempt to put out the fire is unauthorised, but is probably a justified effort to protect my interests. You may also have been motivated by a desire to stop the fire spreading to your house next door, but that does not stop the situation being one of benevolent intervention. Nor does the failure of your intervention; even if my house is completely destroyed, you will still be entitled to claim your fire-fighting expenses. On the other hand, if you negligently used inappropriate means of tackling the fire and made the situation worse, I might have a delictual action against you to compensate me for the loss you have caused me.[2] There is also a link with unjustified enrichment in that if you make a profit from your intervention, you must account to me for it.

The law of benevolent intervention deals with situations very similar to those treated under the heading of enrichments by imposition (above, pp.9–11, 13–15, 43–46). Key differences would include the following:

- in cases of improvements to another's property, the intervener need not be labouring under any error as to ownership or any other ground making the other person's enrichment unjustified, before a claim can be made; nor need the management enrich the other person; and
- in cases of payment of another's debt, the payer who intends to discharge the other's obligation can use benevolent intervention as the basis of recovery if the payment achieves its objective, the claim being for the cost of doing so (which, in money cases, is exactly the same as the amount of the debtor's enrichment).[3] But if the debtor is not absent, ignorant or incapable, or if the payer acted entirely to protect its own interests, then in principle only the enrichment claim is available to that party.

Given the idea that enrichment claims are "subsidiary", only for use where there is no other legal remedy (above, pp.53–54), it would seem that a claim should be made in benevolent intervention first if possible.

There can be enrichment elements in cases of benevolent intervention. Where a party has managed another's affairs but not all the requirements of benevolent intervention are met—for example, the intervener acted entirely in its own interests—there may still be a claim for expenses but it is capped by the amount of any enrichment gained by the principal as a result of the intervention. Other examples include the intervener acting

---

[1] Benevolent intervention should not be confused with agency of necessity (for which see J.J. Gow, *The Mercantile and Industrial Law of Scotland* (1964), pp.521–522). There is some sign of such confusion in *Bank of Scotland v MacLeod Paxton Woolard & Co*, 1998 S.L.T. 258.

[2] See *Kolbin v Kinnear*, 1931 S.C. (H.L.) 128; *Stair Memorial Encyclopaedia*, Vol.15, para.136.

[3] See, e.g. *Reid v Lord Ruthven* (1918) 55 S.L.R. 616.

against an express prohibition from the principal (although here the claim will be further limited to pre-prohibition expenditure), and the intervener who, thinking to manage his own affairs, finds that in fact the business is that of another.[1] Again, if a intervener is enriched by managing another's affairs, most probably by taking or use of the other's property, he may be liable to reimburse the principal.[2]

Not every legal system recognises the obligation of benevolent intervention. The obvious problem is the encouragement which it may give to those who meddle without authority in other people's business. It is a perfectly tenable view that in general such interference should not impose legally enforceable obligations upon the recipient. On the other hand, it would be a poor kind of society in which people helped each other only when specifically asked or authorised to do so, particularly when the person in difficulty was unable to help him or herself for some reason. The rules of benevolent intervention are intended to distinguish the deserving intervener from the unworthy busybody, and seem to have done so successfully since Roman times.

FURTHER READING

The fullest treatment of benevolent intervention *(negotiorum gestio)* in Scots law is by N.R. Whitty: "Negotiorum Gestio", in *Stair Memorial Encyclopaedia*, Vol. 15 (Law Society of Scotland, 1996), paras 87–143. A study comparing Scots and South African law on the subject is N.R. Whitty and D. van Zyl, "Unauthorized management of affairs *(negotiorum gestio)*", in **Mixed Legal Systems in Comparative Perspective**, R. Zimmermann, D. Visser and K. Reid (eds) (2004), Ch.13. The text of Book V of the DCFR, "Benevolent Intervention in Another's Affairs", is drawn from **Principles of European Law: Benevolent Intervention in Another's Affairs**, C. von Bar (ed) (2006), which contains extensive comparative notes on the subject in European legal systems.

---

[1] See *Stair Memorial Encyclopaedia*, Vol.15, paras 137–141.
[2] See *Stair Memorial Encyclopaedia*, Vol.15, paras 133–135.

QUICK QUIZ

UNJUSTIFIED ENRICHMENT

- How may enrichment by transfer, enrichment by taking, and imposed enrichment be distinguished from each other? Why do these distinctions matter?
- What is:
  (i) indirect enrichment;
  (ii) incidental enrichment?
  In what circumstances is recovery for each:
  (i) allowed;
  (ii) disallowed?
- Which of the Roman law *condictiones* is recognised in the modern Scots law of unjustified enrichment, and what role do they now play? Explain the differences between the main recognised *condictiones*.
- How may the remedies of repetition, restitution and recompense be related to the different kinds of enrichment?
- On what legal grounds may an enrichment be justified?
- When will the law allow a claim for unauthorised intervention in another's affairs?

INDEX